#L♥VE

21st-Century Relationships

Trish Murphy

MERCIER PRESS

IRISH PUBLISHER – IRISH STORY

MERCIER PRESS

Cork

www.mercierpress.ie

© Trish Murphy, 2016

ISBN: 978 1 78117 372 5

10 9 8 7 6 5 4 3 2 1

A CIP record for this title is available from the British Library

Printed and bound in the EU.

For Dan, whose light shines on

Contents

Acknowledgements

Thank you to Mercier Press for asking me to write this book. It set in motion many coffee sessions with wonderful people, during which I asked them what they had encountered in relationships and what they felt were the important points. Interviewees were very open and their trust in me was humbling – I hope I have done them a good service in representing their views and experiences. I thank them hugely for everything.

To my readers Clare, Nathaniel and Billy: I thank you not only for your patience and honesty, but also for your many consoling texts and emails when I felt I was getting nowhere.

My peer group Betty and John were unstintingly supportive in convincing me that I had something worth saying; may we continue to meet for the next twenty years. To all the individuals and couples who have worked with me over the years: your contribution and wisdom are reflected in every page, and my gratitude is eternal.

My family quietly took over tasks and duties so that I could have the space to think and write. To them I owe a debt that will be a joy to repay. To Brendan I can finally say that I am settling into using the word 'husband' and am beginning to understand its meaning after all these years. May there be lots more revelations to come!

Preface

In my professional life, I encounter much suffering that has relationship difficulties at its core. Most people have taken some measures to tackle these issues, and yet numerous couples suffer for many a long year before seeking help. The patterns they wish to address are often ingrained and can be difficult to shift. Changing can be hard, and old patterns don't fall away without notable resistance first. I feel lucky that my chosen field has offered me ongoing training and research into the world of relationships, and I know that my life has benefited enormously as a result. I've often wondered if people could be saved the hardship of years of struggle if they had some feasible answers to meet the challenge of relationships. I've also considered how a practical source of information regarding this challenge could go a long way towards preventing the many issues I deal with every day.

A period of twenty years as a couples psychotherapist has given me access to the range of difficulties that beset relationships, but it has also shown me the astounding resources people have for finding a way through what can appear to be insurmountably problematic situations. My experience is that we, as human beings, are often willing to stretch ourselves beyond what we think is possible in order to keep the love of another. While this does not always work out, knowing that love has this enormous influence is inspiring and might give us the courage to take the risk again with another person.

I had the privilege of interviewing many people who generously participated in the research for this book. I discovered during this process that there is a wealth of information and experience available within each of us and in the people around us, if we have the courage to ask the right questions. During these sessions, many of the interviewees found that what they were saying was enlightening – even to themselves. I learned from this experience that we need to talk more about relationships, in all their aspects, as this discussion can benefit everyone. I hope that you might use this book in this way – that it might spark a conversation between you and your partner or friend, or ignite a discussion that might open new avenues for understanding relationships.

The aim of the book is to provide accessible measures of insight and information for users who wish to overcome challenges in their relationship. I hope that much of the text sounds familiar to readers, and that any insight it contains can be solidified into something practical and applicable.

All the exercises in the book are the result of years of learning and practice in my own life. I can testify to their worth but also to the struggle to keep them as a live and continuous part of my everyday existence. To be alive is to be in a continuous learning situation, and the fun of relationships is you can share that with someone special.

Introduction

I'm gonna love you till the wheels come off.

From 'Picture in a Frame' by Tom Waits[1]

How do we find enduring love? How do we measure success or failure in relationships? What criteria do we use, and can we separate our own sense of well-being and success from that of a relationship? Does a single relationship failure, or a series of them, mean that we should give up, or can we learn from our mistakes and past blunders? What are the traps and issues in modern relationships? How does technology affect us? This book deals with all these subjects. Interviews, anecdotes, media reports, surveys, research and my years of professional experience as a couples therapist all go into the mix of attempting to frame the topic of relationships. As far as possible, the book takes a practical approach, and all the suggestions appear in a clear list in the 'Practical advice and exercises' section at the end of the book.

Relationships are an important topic for all of us as we live our lives out in a variety of complex and varied family, friend-ship, romantic and social arrangements. This book focuses on romantic relationships, but our capacity for these is shaped by all our other relationships, and so we can apply most of the

---

1   Waits, T., 'Picture in a Frame', *Mule Variations* [CD] (ANTI-, 1999).

suggestions to the wider field of our lives. That is to say that if you are not currently in a relationship you can apply most of the practices – with modifications – to all other relationships. Having enduring relationships across the board is a good indicator of your capacity to find enduring love in a romantic setting; the time to put this into practice is now, and not at some future mythical time when the right person or situation arrives.

The first section of the book centres on our own self-development. A familiar comment is 'I want to fix myself before I consider getting into a relationship.' While this has some validity, the chances are that what you need to 'fix' in yourself will be very obvious in any relationship, and – if you are open to it – you can receive a lot of support to address these difficulties through the relationship. For example, it is often through a lover's hands that we discover the contours of our own bodies and the beauty therein. Left to our own devices, we might think our bodies will never be good enough for such intimate scrutiny.

The idea of independence is very strong in our society, as we fear coming across as 'needy'. This can lead to an overly cautious approach to both friendships and intimate relationships. Yet it is through taking the risk of dependence that we receive the reward of being completely accepted for ourselves. Of course, it does not always work out. We can be hurt, but learning how to pick ourselves up, and knowing that we can survive, are important life skills that will enhance our next foray into closeness.

This section also looks at whether we can be happy without intimate relationships. We can gain from *all* our relationship experiences – whether they be work, friendship or intimate associations. Applying this learning should offer us more personal freedom and happiness.

Technology now occupies a huge part of our lives and our relationships. This is reflected in two chapters: Chapter 3 on online dating and Chapter 7 on pornography. As we negotiate relationships in our world, we are likely to encounter technology in many forms. It can have a hugely positive influence in terms of enhancing communication – through, for example, Skype, mobile technology and texting – thus allowing relationships to flourish despite distance or lack of time. However, engaging with the online world in terms of dating can be daunting or discouraging; to assist in this endeavour the book outlines potential research and pitfalls. Porn in relationships is a topic that the media are beginning to cover, but we probably don't yet easily discuss it in our private worlds. However, it can have a big influence on intimacy and deserves further conversation in our private, social and public spheres.

The practical exercises near the back of the book are simple to follow and yet often prove difficult to apply. It is one thing to have knowledge and another to keep it constantly in practice. For example, the first exercise – 'How to argue better' – could save a couple lots of grief and misunderstanding if it is implemented early in the relationship. It helps enormously to discuss, reflect and review your progress with someone who is close to you. In fact, by allowing this support you will already be practising one of the key skills in relationships: to acknowledge vulnerability.

As a popular Ed Sheeran song goes, 'people fall in love in mysterious ways', but that is only part of the story. Staying in love, and creating love, is a continuous, practical activity that can grow, change and develop. There is so much we can do to keep love vibrant. Most of that is within our own control; this should give us a sense of hope when things get difficult. Instead of putting off tackling things with the idea that they will get better with time, we can take the risk of engaging early and saving ourselves a lot of suffering.

But we do not have to reinvent the wheel! We can use the knowledge and research available, and thus avoid having to learn everything from scratch. For example, the research discussed in Chapter 5 on what leads to separation could make people pause to consider how they fight, and offer them an alternative path for grievances.

This book is written from the experience of dealing with problems in relationships, and the aim is that readers can dip into it for a specific purpose, for example, to look up self-confidence or how to get started in a new relationship. The book offers a trek through all the experience and knowledge I've gained from clinical experience, and also from all the contributions and wisdom of others who have had experience of all aspects of relationships, both successful and difficult. The bibliography at the end of the book suggests further reading that is accessible and practical.

Self-development

If I love myself
I love you.
If I love you
I love myself.

From 'Do You Love Me?' by Rumi[1]

Self-awareness and habit

The qualities we need to create and to develop the possibility of enduring love are many, but the starting point is self-awareness. This means that we need to be aware of where we are coming from in a physical, mental and emotional sense, so that we are not just reacting from habit. Just think of how strong some of our habits are, and it becomes clear how ingrained they can be. For example, try getting out of bed earlier in the morning, or giving up eating chocolate or crisps for a week, and you will encounter resistance and struggle. We develop relationship habits in our families, and we all think this is completely normal until someone else bumps up against them – it is only then that we see the habits for what they are. For example, Jake amusedly told

---

1 Rumi, 'Do You Love Me', in Chopra, D. (ed.), *The Love Poems of Rumi* (Harmony Books, New York, 1998), p. 36.

his new wife that her family were obsessed with cleaning up after eating so they could relax, whereas his family relaxed *while* eating. This was funny early in the relationship, but it created a clash later on when the couple had very different ideas about relaxation.

Whatever our parents did or how they behaved was normal for us growing up. We are often very aware of how different we want our romantic relationships to be from what our parents offered – only to find that later we either repeat that very thing or else our childhood response presents a huge difficulty in adult relationships. For example, if your parent never gave you credit or praised you, you may be extremely sensitive to your partner's lack of attention, so you may overreact or attack, even though this response comes from the hurt child you were many years ago. Self-awareness is the starting point for knowing what is really happening. We can develop self-awareness through self-reflection, discussion, enquiry, meditation and reading, among other things. (To help with this, see *Exercise 2: Self-awareness: knowing the state you are in and grounding yourself* in the 'Practical Advice and Exercises' section.)

Most habits are outside our self-awareness, in that we do not notice we are doing this particular habitual thing. Often the stronger the habit, the more buried it is, so it is even more difficult to tackle. Some habits are benign, but many are causing us blocks or serious difficulty. An example is the habit of thinking 'I am not good enough' or 'I have nothing worth saying'. If we are not aware of these habitual thoughts, we might act as if they were true and never discover our true worth. It is only when we can see the habit in operation that we have the chance to challenge it. Of course, the nature of habit is that it is the familiar, easy route, so changing habits will be hard and the process will be fraught with setbacks.

How can I change?

There is no doubt that change and development are desirable. If we want to develop characteristics or qualities that will improve our lives, then it will take consistent practice and reinforcement. The general wisdom is that it takes more than ninety days of consciously putting something into practice before it becomes a habit, so any change will take motivation and effort, and some level of self-discipline. Most of us benefit from having another person supporting us in making any desired change. If possible, tell someone about what changes you want to make. Simply keeping this person informed will make that change more possible.

Because habits are so often hidden from our awareness, it is a great idea to ask people close to us what they think we need to tackle. Because we asked, we are less likely to react defensively and might be curious about how they think we could overcome this particular block. For example, Liz (47) asked her son what habits were bringing her down, and he wrote a long list. On the top were two things that Liz found surprising. He wrote that she became very stressed about anything to do with money or her mother-in-law. She began to consider these and discovered that they were true, so she began to lighten up. Over the years she improved her relationship with both.

We are often very clear about what other people need to address in terms of their lack of awareness. However, it is a good idea to wait until they ask for advice, as our suggestions can otherwise be perceived as criticism.

There is evidence that practising self-awareness in a group setting has more beneficial effects than individual self-awareness, particularly in the early days of practice. Joining a course in mindfulness or a reading group would kick-start the process. The group gives us support when we lose interest, and listening to how others are challenging habits can reveal our own hidden patterns and offer us ideas of how to overcome them. So the group supports the practice and deepens the awareness as we listen to others' experiences and get reinforcement from others' understanding and development.

Risk: the first step towards a relationship

All relationships require risk. There is no way of having a relationship without vulnerability and exposure – you have to allow the other person into your life and under your skin, and this gives them the knowledge and the ability to hurt you. The quality we need to develop to have this capacity for risk is courage (with intelligence). We need courage so that we can, first, understand that we fear being hurt and, second, have the ability to overcome this fear. Our fear can be exaggerated by our past experiences of perhaps choosing badly in love and being rejected, humiliated and even derided. If we let these experiences determine all our future relationships, we will partake only of short, safe relationships – and ultimately non-relationships – such as one-night stands or largely text or email relationships. We have to overcome the fear and let our defences down to have a satisfactory, real and enduring relationship. If we are motivated to overcome the fear in this area of our lives, it will enhance our capacity in all other areas also. Imagine feeling free to express yourself openly and truthfully, rather than defensively or obliquely to protect yourself from hurt. Of course, when we express ourselves openly we need to do this with intelligence and good judgement, but fear will always cloud this ability, so the first task is to practise fearlessness. (See *Exercise 3: Overcoming fear.*)

Will (29) had a number of good but, ultimately, unsuccessful relationships. Recently he met someone online who showed a lot of promise. On their first date, Will decided to take the risk of being honest about his fragile mental health, as he did not want to waste time if this was not acceptable. To his surprise, it elicited total openness on the other side and the relationship blossomed.

When someone has the courage to speak honestly, it often has the effect of inviting the other person into a real conversation, thus beginning a relationship. No one wants fear to run their lives or cloud their communication; yet, without our knowing it, this is exactly what can happen. The fear of rejection or humiliation can block you from being yourself, and you can easily miss or ignore opportunities for connection. It takes strength and courage to risk being genuine, and these are characteristics worth cultivating. Speaking honestly and expressing yourself genuinely, without fear, will require and grow courage and fortitude. We often hold on to past experiences of rejection very tightly. This might make us very risk adverse, but all partners are *not* the same. What we want is to learn from our experiences and trust ourselves to make better choices next time.

Good judgement

We need to see our potential partners clearly, and not through projections or rose-coloured glasses. Our capacity for judgement comes into play here. Many people find that they are surprised by a partner's harshness at the end of a relationship, only to realise, when they really think about it, that this characteristic was always there but they decided to ignore it or act as if it was not present.

Adam (25) returned to his apartment following a week at a music work gig to find his girlfriend gone and a cold note from her saying that their relationship was over. They had been living together for eighteen months. Now Adam can see that this coldness had always been present and that she was acting completely in character, but his desire for romance had made him blind to this. He reckons that he knew for six months that the relationship was doomed, but he pushed his knowledge and intelligence out of the way in favour of the notion, 'I can make this work if I believe enough in it.'

Our desire for a relationship – combined with the fear of loneliness – can block us from seeing the obvious. And sometimes we choose to ignore the obvious. Wendy (32) did this when she chose a man who was handsome but mean. 'I was so flattered by his attention and I was getting older, so

I ignored the fact that he would complain about buying a round of drinks,' she explains. 'Now I am driven crazy by it.'

We need to access our intelligence and capacity for perception (see *Exercise 4: Accessing intelligence*), so that we are dealing with reality and not fantasy. For example, if we are fully aware that our partners have no empathy, we will not be hurt when they act in very uncaring ways. We will know that this is how they are, but that they need to develop empathy if they are going to continue to be in a relationship. Anyone can develop emotional intelligence and learn empathy if they are motivated enough to seek them out.[2]

There are fifteen competencies identified in emotional intelligence tests – these are tests that complement the intelligence quotient (IQ) test. While our IQ remains largely static throughout our lives, we can develop and grow our emotional intelligence. Research in emotional intelligence demonstrates that we can develop all the emotional competencies through practice, and indeed these capabilities grow naturally until we reach about fifty years of age. It can happen that when we are a year or more into a relationship we wonder why we didn't see the obvious earlier on; often this is because we have chosen not to. The other person hasn't changed, and it is not their fault that we put him or her on a pedestal. It is up to us to see our partners as they are and not as we would like them to be.

The old saying 'love is blind' comes into play here. To use another cliché that nevertheless remains pertinent, we need

---

2   Goleman, D., *Emotional Intelligence* (Bantam Books, New York, 1995).

to use our heads along with our hearts to make a decision about whom to get into a relationship with. However, to be fair, many people behave very well in the early stages of infatuation and it is only later that they relapse into their old ways of being. This is when an opportunity for appraisal presents itself: is this person capable of development and, if so, are we willing to put the effort in to help the person reach his or her potential? Can we take the risk of losing the relationship if we challenge the difficulties? If we are not usually good at judging people or have a history of being unassertive in our friendships, we might need to work on trusting our judgements and being more forceful in our assertions. It is often the case that years after a relationship or friendship ends, we discover that all the necessary information was present from the beginning, if only we had been prepared to see it. Being aware of our blind spots is key; again, we may need to check in with our nearest and dearest to see if we are on the right track.

Molly (41) married her husband against the advice and concerns of her friends. At the time she thought she was lucky to find someone to love her, and she overlooked his self-centredness and addictive characteristics. Years later, when these characteristics were in full force, she realised that her desire to be married had caused her to overlook the evidence of her husband's personality and to ignore the input of her friends.

Self-confidence
Self-confidence is a highly attractive quality in a life partner,

and self-confidence also means that we do not allow ourselves to be demeaned in any relationship. Many of us have a strange relationship with self-esteem in that we often try to act with confidence while hiding the truth of our vulnerability. However, this is no good to us; *acting* confident is not the real thing and it encourages the fear of being found out. This creates an ever-present barrier between us and our partners.

Self-confident people are those who like being themselves, present themselves as they really are to the world and like being in their own skin. Most children are born with self-confidence. This can slowly leak away or be covered over with learned ideas or notions, such as 'I am not as smart, beautiful, clever, thin, successful, etc., as other people.' These sentences or thoughts can become an ever-present accompaniment to living, and after many years of practising them, we believe them to be true. Our response may be to hide these convictions and pretend we don't care. Or we may block anyone from discovering our true (messy) selves. We seek to have someone in our lives who truly knows us and accepts us for who we are, but then we fear that they will reject us as unacceptable. We may also get angry at not being accepted, but the starting point is to risk expressing our true selves to our partners and others.

How to become more confident
Developing confidence requires us to become aware of – and then to let go of – the ideas, thoughts and notions that block or cover over our true selves. Be present, be authentic and

risk being honest, as this is the pathway to being your natural self. (See *Exercise 5: Developing confidence*, which offers a practice you can adopt for uncovering the blocks to confidence and developing self-respect.)

Practising honest expression is very challenging, and we also need to do it while taking the other person into account. For example, it is important to express being upset, but the way in which we say it must not demean the other person. If you start a sentence with 'You are such a …', this will not allow the other person to understand your position and he or she is likely to dismiss you. Instead, begin with 'I'm feeling …' and ask the other person's opinion. Being heard is an important part of growing self-confidence, so it is essential to speak in a way that allows the other person to understand you fully.

Good decision-making

The ability to make good decisions is another personal quality that is crucial in relationships. If we cannot make a decision, then a relationship might not start at all, or become stalled at some point, and so suffer from inertia or lack of momentum. Can you imagine having to make a conscious decision every day about whether to go to work or not? This would lead to exhaustion, and your workplace would probably get rid of you pretty quickly. The reason that we do well at work is that we make a decision, say yes to the job offer and then commit to the job until it becomes clear to us that we need a change. Relationships need the same trajectory if they are to develop and thrive.

If, for example, you have a pattern of a three-week date period, after which you automatically look for an exit, this denies you the ability to use good judgement in the relationship. Instead, the habit of looking for an exit after such a short space of time precludes the possibility of allowing more time for the connection to develop, as it would, for example, with people who fall in love at work after a long time of knowing each other. In fact it will mean that an exit is the only outcome possible. Moira (27) says she can't understand why relationships don't work out for her. She muses, 'They always end after a month, and I think it's because I project forward to the future and decide it's better to get out now and save myself the pain and trouble later.' She exits the relationship based on the fear that it will cause her hurt later, rather than on good judgement in the present.

Timely decision-making

Indecision can be chronic and caused by fear of regret, or fear of being trapped, or missing out, or many other possibilities. This means that no relationship can develop, and that the outcome is always the same: indecision causes monitoring, evaluation and, ultimately, endings, as the partner eventually cannot put up with the uncertainty.

Sometimes we try to make a decision on a relationship before we have sufficient knowledge; for example, we start thinking about living together before we know each other well enough to say we are a couple. This is insulting to our intelligence, as we do not have enough information and knowledge to make a proper decision for ourselves. The opposite also applies: we go past the decision point in the agony of 'what ifs', and so miss the opportunity to grow something worthwhile and valuable.

We need to practise good decision-making in the right moment. We can do this in all kinds of ways, for example by deciding to change something small – such as leaving on time to meet someone, and not ten minutes later – and following through on it completely. If you do this, it will give you confidence and faith in yourself, and you will feel lighter and more successful. Simply remembering how significant that friend is will stop you checking your email before you leave. We would never be late for a job interview because we know how important it is; we should give meeting our friends and families the same amount of importance, and then we will be on time.

How to be good at decision-making

Try to follow what you say; don't say one thing and mean another. For example, if you say, 'I love being with you,' do not then spend the night thinking, 'What if this is not the right person?' If you make good decisions for yourself today, the chances of making good decisions for yourself in five years' time are assured. Trust that you have the resources and capacity to tackle whatever you need to face in the future, and do not let fear be your major deciding factor. While you need some fear to help you with decisions – for example, when to cross a road – having faith in yourself and in your capacity offers you far better options than using fear alone as the deciding tool.

Follow-through is an important part of gaining confidence in your decision-making – for example, if you say, 'We will meet next week,' and you follow through by actually calling the person to arrange it. If you tell someone that you will do something for him or her, follow through on it. By practising follow-through, you will begin to refine what you say and do. You will offer to meet someone again only if you mean it, and this will stop you saying things you do not mean. (See *Exercise 6: Decision-making.*)

Self-development

Of course all the qualities outlined above are worthy of books in their own right:

- Being self-aware and aware of habits

- Taking risks

- Facing fear

- Growing self-confidence

- Developing good judgement

- Honing the capacity of decision-making and follow-through

Many of us have already had experiences of and forays into developing these skills, and the idea here is to hone them and clarify them to remind ourselves to keep developing them. For example, many of us have had to overcome fear when giving a presentation or a speech. We take risks in changing jobs or locations, and we know that our confidence grows when we feel less burdened by self-commentary – the non-stop, largely negative commentary we make about ourselves to ourselves, which is a burden in that it creates tension and emotional disturbance. We know that we can have excellent judgement when helping others with their problems, and we have experience of making clear and easy decisions. Now we can further develop these qualities with deliberation and practice.

If we grow these qualities, this instantly enhances our capacity for relationships and strengthens our ability to care for and choose well for ourselves. The tendency is always to look for the other person to change for things to improve, but in fact the person we can change – and whom we can be successful with – is ourselves. If you want to know if you are succeeding in growing any of the qualities, the best measure is if you are feeling lighter and less bothered. This is highly motivating!

Most of us have had some success with tackling these issues in one way or other, but it is easy to let the effort slip, and old habits can resurface almost imperceptibly. It is probable that we will always meet further challenges in these areas and will continue to grow in knowledge and capacity in dealing with them as long as we are alive. As novelist Tom Robbins writes in *Still Life with Woodpecker*:

When we're incomplete, we're always searching for somebody to complete us. When, after a few years or a few months of a relationship, we find that we're still unfulfilled, we blame our partners and take up with somebody more promising. This can go on and on – series polygamy – until we admit that while a partner can add sweet dimensions to our lives, we, each of us, are responsible for our own fulfilment. Nobody else can provide it for us, and to believe otherwise is to delude ourselves dangerously and to program for eventual failure every relationship we enter.[3]

---

3   Robbins, T., *Still Life with Woodpecker* (Bantam Books, New York, 1980), p. 157.

2

Romantic relationships

There is no doubt that seeking relationships, and being in enjoyable relationships, is not only good for us but is a survival skill. Being in a long-term relationship is linked to living longer and more healthily. We come from ancestors who were very successful at social living, so we are structured to be communal in nature. The role of romantic love is relatively new in the scheme of things; the luxury of choosing a partner for reasons of love came into vogue only a century or two ago. Before this, families made the choice, which was based on social, economic and practical factors. Even now, the choice of a life partner in many parts of the world continues to be based successfully on social, academic, economic and companionship status, but in the western world most people would not choose this way unless they had the 'love' ingredient as well.

It is hard to clarify what the term 'love' means, as we usually feel it when we are in the throes of infatuation, but we realise that it is not the real deal until later, when we really like and admire the person we have lusted after. In *The Science of Happily Ever After*, Ty Tashiro says that most Americans describe 'liking and lust' as the two ingredients of a lasting romantic relationship.[1]

---

1   Tashiro, T., *The Science of Happily Ever After: What Really Matters in the Quest for Enduring Love* (Harlequin, Don Mills, 2014), p. 11.

Kindness + loyalty + fairness + lust = romantic love

A starting point for looking at successful relationships is to view how children choose friendships. Children make these choices based on kindness, loyalty and fairness. If we add lust to that, then there is a possibility of longevity.[2] Imagine saying I am really into that person, but I don't like spending time with him/her. This would not make sense; our actions must be congruent with our intentions, and then the relationship is secure.

Kindness

Kindness is consistently rated as a huge factor in relationships: if someone is unkind to us in private or public it does not bode well for the relationship. Kindness means our partners are able to focus on us, perceive our needs and act on them. We are in their circle of attention and are able to trust that the attention is valid and not fake. If someone fakes kindness, we feel it immediately as a sort of dismissal, and our reaction is to avoid that person. In a recent survey of 'enduring love', 4,494 UK participants rated relationships across a range of topics. In support of the 'kindness factor' participants related the following:

- Saying 'thank you' and thoughtful gestures were prized most highly by all participants. Recognition of the time and effort required to complete the everyday mundane

---

2   Marshall, A., *I Love You but I'm Not in Love with You: Seven Steps to Saving Your Relationship* (Bloomsbury, London, 2007).

tasks which underpin relationships and the smooth running of a household were also prized.

• Surprise gifts and small acts of kindness were valued highly, with a 'cup of tea' being singled out as a significant sign of their partner's appreciation. Bouquets of flowers and boxes of chocolates were seen as less important than the thoughtfulness behind the gesture.[3]

Further research into kindness suggests that it is located in the smallest of couple exchanges, a turn of the head, a mumbled comment or a focused eye gaze: 'The smallest moments told an important story. The particular ways partners responded to each other's bids for connection forged the relative strength of their future relationship and intimacy, which in turn shaped how well they managed conflict.'[4] Being responsive to your partner in the smallest of ways seems to have a huge influence on the relationship. This is in stark contrast to the belief that couples need a lot of time to work on the relationship. Kindness is expressed in gestures and moments of attention.

Attention is key to relationships, and in the early stages of a relationship there is huge focus on the loved person – every gesture, word and look is given enormous time and

---

3 Gabb, J., Klett-Davies, M., Fink, J. and Thomae, M., 'Findings, Executive Summary', *Enduring Love? Couple Relationships in the 21st Century* (Open University Press, Milton Keynes, 2013), pp. 5–6.
4 Gottman, J. and Schwartz Gottman, J., 'Lessons from the Love Lab: The Science of Couples Therapy', *Psychotherapy Networker*, Nov/Dec 2015, p. 41.

energy. But it can happen that when the relationship is solidified in some way that consideration can wane, and very quickly the spark can be lost and the relationship comes into question. There are practical ways of keeping the focus alive through text messages, conversation, demonstrating interest and voicing appreciation, but at the core of it is giving attention fully to the other person – even if that is only for a few minutes. Half-hearted attention can be demeaning. It can also lead to all sorts of arguments to secure the other's consideration. The difficulty is that we give the least attention to those closest to us, as we assume we know what is going on. There are practical ways to become better at giving attention and taking this on is an expression of commitment to the relationship (see *Exercise 7: Attention*).

Strangely, our work colleagues and customers often get more of our attention than those closest to us, and then we are surprised to find that our relationships have deteriorated. Kindness and attention require a practical input in the form of communication, time and interest. Another quotation from the *Enduring Love* survey makes this clear:

> Talking and listening were appreciated as one of the most effective means by which couples came to understand, reassure and comfort each other. Arguments and poor communication, notably around money issues, were frequently cited as one of the least liked aspects of [the] relationship.
>
> Being 'best friends' with your partner ranked very highly amongst all women and men, with the type of friendship being used to signify emotional closeness. Respect, encouragement

and kindness were valued features of such relationships, together with a confidence that concerns and problems could be shared.[5]

Loyalty

Loyalty is another quality that is crucial to relationships. In romantic relationships this includes fidelity or loyalty to the partner. Many of the people interviewed said that they took fidelity as a given, even in long-distance relationships: for example, Clodagh (29) said, 'We never discussed it. There was never any question of fidelity not being there. You just assume it.'

Loyalty means that you can trust the other person to choose you first. When you were a child, you expected your best friend to choose you over other friends, to want to spend most of their available free time with you, and, if possible, to choose to sit beside you if a seat was available. In the same way, loyalty in romantic relationships implies that you can assume your place at the top of the other person's hierarchy of important people, and you need evidence of this. If this slips, and there is evidence that you are not the most important person in the life of your partner, then this becomes a source of grievance and difficulty. However, how we demonstrate loyalty probably stems from our families, and we first need to know ourselves what our usual demonstration of loyalty is (for example, it might be turning up for lunch on Sundays, phoning once a year, or offering financial support if it is

---

5   Gabb *et al.* (2013), p. 5.

needed). Then comes the difficult part of matching our sense of loyalty to our partner's.

Bill and Linda had very different forms of showing how much they meant to each other. Linda wanted birthday presents and regular tokens of affection at proper times, such as Christmas. Bill felt that was too kitsch, and he would only provide presents when they were unexpected. This led to friction and undermined Linda's fragile faith in the relationship. If you and your partner have discussed how to show loyalty and you can accept your partner's version of this – even if it is not in the form that you would like – trust can begin to grow, and it can form a strong base for the relationship.

Loyalty is not offering our own version of what we have grown up with, but putting the effort into meeting the other person's needs. Relationships stretch us beyond our self-centred limits, and love makes us generous and kind. Indeed, loyalty for life can be a very tough proposition, and one which is challenged in unexpected ways.

Tom, a man in his late twenties, found that loyalty and fidelity needed redefining in his life, as his partner did not see sex with other people as challenging to the relationship, while Tom did. Despite this, Tom chose to stay in the relationship, commenting:

> I started to re-evaluate my own approach to relationships, to look at my own values on sex and the importance I placed on it. Within a year I had come around to departing from the traditional model ... I found that I was holding on to a

moral code that did not fit my liberal views. It is a completely different relationship now. He started having sex for the right reasons and I stopped hating him for the wrong reasons.

Honest conversations and enquiry about what loyalty and fidelity mean are hugely important, as we can assume a certain immovable moral code only to find that our assumptions are incorrect. This is particularly needed when there are cultural or religious differences in the relationship, as we need to bring assumptions to the surface and accommodate them. Loyalty also involves challenge. Unquestioned loyalty does not suffice. If our partner is being rude or obnoxious, loyalty requires that we stand by him or her; however, love gives us permission to challenge the behaviour, as we know that our beloved can be a better person than this. In fact, trusting that the other person has your back can allow you to tolerate and challenge all kinds of disagreements and differences. (Chapter 5 will offer more discussion on this and on how to argue.) The expectation of loyalty and fidelity for life is one that needs constant revisiting and attention, as there will be threats over the lifetime of a long relationship. Chapter 8 discusses cheating and affairs, but it is important to acknowledge here that when loyalty in a relationship comes under threat in any way, the fundamentals of the relationship come under scrutiny. This can signal the relationship's demise.

Fairness

Fairness and reciprocity are central to the maintenance of any relationship. Our sense of fairness is most likely innate, in that we know when there is an imbalance or when things start to slip into injustice. This is often felt in long-distance relationships when perhaps one person is left carrying the family load while the other person lives a single life abroad. It can also arise when one person feels he or she is carrying the entire financial load for the family and is unappreciated by the partner in the relationship.

Josh (50) worked for many years in South America with only quarter-yearly contact with his wife and children, but he was very adaptable when he returned home and his wife took on an international job. It felt 'fair':

> We are very good at, and used to, living apart. We have a system … we'd open a bottle of wine and always find time for each other. The passion is still there all these years later – it comes from a certain kind of imbalance. I'm the glue holding things together while my wife travels.

Josh was able to adapt to the new position of his wife taking on the role of the major breadwinner and the international travel that this entails, because he felt that it was fair in the sense that she had tolerated his travels for work at an earlier phase.

There is no doubt that all relationships involve sacrifice, and this surprisingly enhances the relationship: think of the sacrifices it takes to become a parent and how delighted people are in this role! Sacrifices – such as giving up your own family and friends to go and live in the country of your partner's choice, or moving to another location to further your partner's career – can be relationship-enhancing choices. However, a lack of reciprocity over the course of the relationship can create a sense of imbalance that can be hard to repair. We use language such as 'I'm doing all the giving and they are doing all the taking' to express what we feel to be a lack of equity, but it is more complicated than that. Fairness does not mean fifty–fifty in terms of housework and the like. Instead, both people have to feel that there is justice in the relationship; for example, one person does all the housework and the other is very appreciative and provides all the financial resources.

Jake and Loren found that after ten years together and juggling different countries, universities and careers, they decided to make 'decisions based on the relationship' rather than on their individual needs. This did not mean that their focus on each career stopped, but they agreed on relationship-building rules such as spending summers together. They were constantly following one of their careers and were very conscious that they would give the other person's career (and resultant country of choice) priority in the next round of decisions they would make. The relationship depended on fairness in supporting one person's potential and dreams, and sacrifice where one person had to make the less desirable choice for a period of time – without this the relationship would not have survived.

Fairness in the normal daily activities can be a source of irritation, but actually it can point to underlying difficulties or inequalities in the relationship. For example, couples can fight over who does what in terms of housework, but often they are checking out the underlying values and principles on which the relationship sits. If they do not have a solid sense that the foundations of the relationship are unmoving, then the tiny inequalities of daily life can expose this fissure and signal that a reassessment is in order. Rows over who empties the dishwasher often signal that one person feels less than important in the relationship, and the resultant sense of unfairness leads to anger and accusation. Conversations about long-term plans for meeting the needs of both people are imperative. These need to happen regularly, to ensure that the relationship is not meeting one person's dreams while the other's are ignored.

Children are often very clear about these issues. They can usually identify unfairness with enormous clarity – however, we need to ask them for their opinion, as they do not usually volunteer these comments. They can spot if someone is doing the lion's share of the household work and they know if change is needed, but they will need encouragement to voice their wisdom. As individuals we need to promote self-awareness for our own well-being, but couples can also benefit from asking family and friends to assess the relationship. We are not always the best judges of the success of our relationships:

> On average, your friends and your family know best. A number of cleverly designed studies have asked partners in romantic relationships and their friends or family about the couple's degree of love and commitment, and the likelihood that their relationship will endure months later or even

culminate in marriage. Across these studies, partners in the relationship report inflated views of the degree of love and commitment in the relationship compared to the ratings from friends or family … Thus it is no surprise that we have all seen situations in which everybody knows that a friend's relationship is a complete disaster, except for the friend in the relationship.[6]

Lust

The extra ingredient in a romantic relationship is lust. Without this the relationship will struggle. The next chapter will discuss lust and attraction, but as an essential factor in enduring relationships it needs to be highlighted here. Many people will have the experience of falling in love and not be able to take their hands off each other for the first year or two, and then discover that this ingredient has all but totally disappeared in later years. Many lament its demise, but others take it as the normal track for relationships. Rarely, however, do both partners agree with the level of desire in the relationship. The familiar phrase 'I love you but I'm not in love with you' will have reverberated through many a break-up, or indeed many a marriage.

Can we keep the initial stages of lust throughout the long life of a relationship? How important is affection and intimacy to a relationship? Very important, it would seem, from conversations with many couples and individuals. All the people interviewed suggested that intimacy is one of the

---

6   Tashiro (2014), p. 169.

core features of a relationship; all understood that intimacy changes from the urgency of the early relationship, but that it provides a sort of cement for the tough times ahead. Liz (54) explains:

> During our twenty-eight years together, our sex lives have gone through many periods – there were times when it seemed like too much trouble and I'd have preferred watching TV but we kept at it as we had an instinct that if we gave it up we might lose it altogether. I am so glad we did as now it has evolved into something great – fun, connecting and joyous and even a bit bold – I am so enjoying it now.

Like everything else in life, if we want to keep or develop something, we need to practise it regularly. The initial attraction signals that there is a chemistry that works, but if you let it slide, it can disappear very easily and it can be difficult to resurrect. Chapter 6 looks at sex and intimacy in relationships, and exercises in the 'Practical advice and exercises' section can help to re-enliven an intimate relationship.

The quest for enduring love in the twenty-first century is set amidst the reality of huge relationship break-ups, separations and divorce. We have more knowledge now of what an enduring relationship can do for us as individuals, for children and for communities, and yet such relationships can elude even the most determined of people. If we can find and sustain love, we are free to venture out into the world, take risks and experiment with life, knowing that we can return and be accepted and loved wholly for who we are. It is a quest worth seeking.

3

Getting into relationships and the online world

Technology has changed relationships in many ways but the area of most change is in how we get into them. Twenty years ago, online dating was for people who were either very computer literate or had exhausted all other means of meeting a potential mate. Now, online dating has become the norm; the younger population find it almost commonplace, but there are difficulties and barriers for those not as comfortable with conducting personal business online. For many people, college years or late teens and early twenties provide them with huge possibilities for dating as they naturally mingle with lots of potential romantic partners. However, following this time (or indeed during this time) the possibility of meeting partners can decrease very quickly. Lives become extremely busy, and the traditional methods of meeting new single people – such as at clubs or sports or dances – are either not available or do not fit with people's lives.

For people who are re-entering the dating scene following a long period in a relationship, engaging with the online world can be quite a scary concept. However, engaging with technology is probably the best method to find other singletons of any age group and demographic, so putting aside resistance and getting in front of the computer is a step towards a possible relationship.

Our capacity for judging whether someone is a match for us still requires face-to-face meetings. Technology provides us with only a two-dimensional version of someone, but to get to this stage we need potential suitors, and should try all methods. Many single people have very full social lives with lots of family, friends and events; they therefore hardly have a weekend free to focus on meeting a mate. While this is a fulfilling life, it will not create a romantic relationship (unless you are very lucky), so getting involved in meeting new single people of appropriate age is something to be developed. Sarah (50) has been online dating for some time and met her full-time partner online about a year ago. She says that there are many barriers to online dating: the time it absorbs, the past experiences and the 'sifting through' that is necessary. It is important to realise that the whole population of Ireland is not the size of a 'decent US city'; it can feel like putting an advert up in a small town – everyone knows very quickly. The 'fear of meeting someone I know' is very relevant to Ireland in a way that would not happen in the USA.

However, in the past, single people went to the dance halls and the local community knew of their search for love. The search space is different nowadays, but there is still no avoiding people knowing that we are in the market for a relationship, and we need to face this fear and challenge it fairly quickly. Clodagh, a twenty-nine-year-old Irish woman living in New York, says that online dating is the standard, and that she has heard the statement 'Would you believe we met in real life?' to indicate just how normal it is to go to the Internet to source a date. As she has very little time, she organises dates over coffee; if she feels it is not going to work out, she ends it very quickly. No one is upset about this, and there is 'no stigma at all' to the shortness of the encounter. She worries that when she comes back to Ireland she will find the dating game to be very different:

> My whole generation have left Ireland. I feel if I was to go home now, I'd have difficulty finding someone to be compatible with. New Yorkers are so up front I don't think I'd know if an Irish man was asking for a date or not.

Ben (35) says that he uses Tinder (a dating app) to meet women occasionally, but he does not see it as a precursor to relationships. He says that he has a three-date rule – if there is no spark after the third date, then he stops meeting up. He says that he has little 'motivation as I do not feel the need or urgency' for a relationship. He sees fun as the major motivating factor and does not believe in 'dating for the sake of it'. Alexander (in his 30s) says that he has had very little success in trying to find a relationship by meeting women in pubs, and the relationships he has had have not worked out: 'She took me for granted and was too casual about it all.' He feels that he will not seriously seek a relationship until he has his career sorted, and so will continue to meet women in pubs. He won't go online, as he feels he is not ready to commit to anything yet.

Three-date rule

The three-date rule is something that crops up a lot. It might be very sensible, but there are many people who fall in love in the workplace and only come to realise the depth of emotion following a long connection. You may need a more flexible approach, so you can assess each case separately – sometimes the three-date rule is the right one and sometimes it could take seven dates to get to know someone well enough to make a decision.

There are no real rules to guarantee success in finding a relationship. There are, however, very good guidelines about how to give yourself the best chance of success in at least getting dates.

Creating a profile

Daisy Buchanan's book *Meeting Your Match* is an excellent guide to beginning online dating. It covers everything from creating a profile and taking a photo, to where to have the first date, among other things.[1] Buchanan has also made these very wise comments in an interview:

- You need to be absolutely secure in the knowledge that you are an attractive and interesting romantic proposition. Be in the right frame of mind before you write your profile.

- You need to keep plodding through and meeting each new challenge with a nod and a giggle. The more people you meet the more you'll learn.

---

1 Buchanan, D., *Meeting Your Match* (Carlton Books, London, 2015).

- Be as honest as possible. Online it's easier to fake a profile and present a façade ... Be kind to people online and remember that we are all human.

- Work the buddy system, so when you're at the moment of actually meeting up with someone you've met online, you get your buddy to read the exchanges first, to get an objective second opinion.

- Meeting online, then having a coffee with the person and deciding where to go from there is less heart-breaking than meeting someone in a pub, then going on six dates before you realise that you don't like each other at all.[2]

Advice for online daters

'Dating in a Digital World' authors Finkel, Eastwick, Karney, Reis and Sprecher have conducted research into the world of online dating.[3] The following points summarise their advice on what to do:

- Set limits for yourself – too much choice can produce choice overload, undermining our ability to make good decisions.

- Online daters choosing from a small rather than a large batch of potential partners are more likely to enjoy

---

2 In an interview with Kate Holmquist: Holmquist, K., 'How to Find Love Online', *The Irish Times*, 10 February 2015, p. 11.
3 Finkel, E. J., Eastwick, P. W., Karney, B. R., Reis, H. T. and Sprecher, S., 'Dating in a Digital World', *Scientific American Mind*, Vol. 23, No. 4, Sept/Oct 2012, pp. 26–33.

the person with whom they end up sharing a candlelit dinner.

- Remain aware of how many profiles you have scanned in a browsing session and impose a time limit. View profiles in manageable clusters and consider reaching out to, say, one out of every twenty users.

- Online daters typically aim too high. Typically daters seek partners by searching through profiles using attributes such as income and hair colour, as opposed to arguably more important factors, such as a sense of humour or rapport.

- The faster the reply the more likely that reciprocal communication will continue. If you sense a spark, don't play hard to get.

- Don't wait too long to set up a date. Research shows that although a small amount of emailing or chatting online can increase attraction, too much of it tends to instil overly specific expectations.

- Even though our decision-making falters under trying conditions, it is worth noting that we are actually quite skilled at deducing certain personality characteristics from sparse amounts of information.

One added piece of advice from Sarah (50) is this: if in doubt, offer to meet the potential person for coffee near where they live as 'this will weed out the marrieds as they will not want to be seen close to home'. She also says that being 'honest' and 'clear about what kind of relationship you are interested in' will save time and energy. She warns women about believing they 'can change the person with time'. Many people are seeking a relationship following the ending of a marriage or a long-term relationship; they are, perhaps, acting as they would when they were last seeking a relationship in their late teens. Sarah says that she finds some of these profiles are looking for a mate (as in friend) to have a fun time with, and they are not actually being realistic about the commitment that a romantic relationship requires.

Another issue is that we are often far more likely to disclose a lot about ourselves when we are online, and this can create a false intimacy. If the relationship continues in a virtual form online, it can feel very intimate and close, but this can be deceiving – when we meet the potential partner in person we might find that it is difficult to correlate the online relationship with the live one. At least twice, James (31) found that he met people online whom he thought would be long-term partners. The disclosure was awesome and the sense of connection huge. However, when they met in person, there was not only awkwardness, but it was also difficult to associate the virtual person with the real one. Now he arranges to meet potential partners in the flesh early in the contact, as this avoids unnecessary disappointment and disillusionment.

The date

It is important to think about and plan the date. If someone has written in their profile that they are 'passionate about life', then the date should demonstrate that. Clodagh says that she has gone on a rock-climbing first date and she appreciated the effort that went into planning it. Tony (23) says that he does a little 'homework' before the date: 'I read up on current affairs or what's new on HBO, so that the conversation won't lag and I can keep it light and interesting.' But no matter how well the first date goes, sometimes that is also the end. Amy (32) says that 'you have to be thick-skinned for Internet dating and be in a good head space; you can think you are getting on great with someone and then you never hear from them again.'

If there is too big a break between dates, then problems can arise. Brenda (23) struggled to make a relationship work, but 'only meeting once every two weeks made even my most optimistic hopes seem ridiculous – he simply did not show enough interest to keep it alive.'

Many people give up after a period of disillusionment or failure when they try online dating, but real successes do happen – persistence, enthusiasm and gaining wisdom all bear fruit. Imagine giving up training for the marathon after three weeks – there would be no possibility of getting over the end line. Most things worth having require energy; putting effort into seeking a life partner is putting substance behind a belief that life lived in a partnership is better than life lived on your own. If this is your view, it's a worthwhile aim.

The reason we want to be in a relationship is that we benefit from it in so many ways; we are healthier, live longer, can share our lives, have tons of affection and keep loneliness at bay. Being in a relationship is also a developmental stage, in that we become more generous and kind, and we have someone to both support and push us to reach our potential. This is not to say that getting into a relationship is the end of the process – as in Hollywood movies when the music swells and credits roll – but, rather, it is the beginning of something: the challenges will stretch and define us and we might actually experience growth. Dating is only the first step in an interesting and compelling journey.

Pitfalls

The online dating world has some pitfalls. One is the probability that someone is connecting with you for a casual sexual hook-up. While many people might want this, it can also be distressing to others. Be upfront with your expectations, so that the other person can't misread them. Another pitfall is the obsessive nature of apps such as Tinder, as this quotation in *Vanity Fair* indicates: 'Tinder sucks, they say. But they don't stop swiping.'[4] Even when people are dating, they can continue to check their online account, and this is often ruinous to the blossoming of the relationship. Cathy (26) said:

> We were on our fifth date and it was going well. When I came back from a trip to the loo, I saw that he was on Tinder swiping right [offering a potential contact to the viewer] – I felt so cross and worried that I was not enough for him.

Handling the lack of response to your online presence can

---

4   Sales, N. J., 'Tinder is the Night', *Vanity Fair*, September 2015, p. 141.

also be difficult and perceived as rejection, but no response could simply mean that you need help with your profile or your own responses. Although many people give up online dating following a few bad experiences, there is enough evidence from couples for whom it *has* worked to make this means of dating a worthwhile endeavour.

Attraction

The spark of attraction needs to be present for both people. Almost everyone acknowledges that if that is missing, then the relationship can't proceed. However, once the spark is there, then developing an interest in the other person – and giving attention and time to that interest – seems to give life and hope to the burgeoning relationship.

Ty Tashiro delves into what we look for in a partner and the problems associated with that: 'Regardless of where people meet, whether it's at work, the park or the church, they often narrow down the field of potential mates based on physical attractiveness.'[5] This lingering tendency to choose a partner based on physical attractiveness is not particularly surprising, given that for most of human history reproductive success was based on having a healthy partner. The archetypal figures of desire are the man with a V-shaped body and a woman with an attractive hip-to-waist ratio. In the quest for enduring love, however, these may not be useful as the sole deciding factor. Lust and infatuation can blind us, and we need to apply our reason and intelligence to choosing

5   Tashiro (2014), p. 79.

a partner with whom love can flourish over decades. Tashiro adds, 'All heart and little use of one's head is a recipe for disaster. The way people find enduring love is by applying both heartfelt intuition and clear reason.'[6]

This difficulty finds a home in online dating, as most judgement goes into finding a physically attractive person – possibly leaving unattended the most enduring characteristics of a potential partner. In fact, most people lie a little online: they might add centimetres to height and take kilograms off weight. Therefore we should exercise prudence until we know more about the other person. The difficulty then is in dating someone who attracts you, while also checking on characteristics such as a sense of humour and similar philosophical notions and interests. Assessing these will take face-to-face interaction.

What creates attraction?

What creates attraction for us? How can we improve our chances of attracting someone with whom we might consider spending our lives? It is essential to consider these questions.

On a very primitive level, we are attracted to health, so someone who glows with vitality, fitness and energy is very appealing to us – perhaps subconsciously we think the person might have good DNA to pass on to our offspring. Thinness doesn't equal healthiness; people of any size who are lively and vigorous will draw others towards them.

The next most attractive thing in a partner is confidence:

---

6   *Ibid.*, p. 106.

we are very attracted to people who like being themselves, who are happy in their own skin and who turn their attention outwards. We don't like spending much time with people who focus inwards towards self-criticism; we love spending time with people who are interested in us and in our lives. Attraction increases when a partner, or potential partner, sees the object of desire doing something they are really good at. Therefore it is a good idea to invite a potential partner to an event at which you are performing or helping out – though not on a first date. This allows the person to see you at your best, thus increasing your attractiveness.

A person looking for a partner often has a stipulation that the partner is steady and is a serious player in the world. Amy (32) says that while looks and health are important, 'a guy's job matters. Without being a snob, it would be the first thing I look at. I'd be attracted to intelligence and ambition.' Laura (29) agrees: 'Looks have become less important. It's now about the long term. I want someone to be stable, someone with a career. Knowing what they want to do with their life is a very attractive quality.'

But using wealth or resources as a basis for a relationship also has its limitations, as findings show: 'Marital satisfaction depends mostly upon the absence of some economic hardships, such as falling below the poverty line, unemployment, foreclosures or large amounts of debt, and once those economic hardships are averted, there is a diminishing return on wealth.'[7] Having money is important, but it seems having

---

7   *Ibid.*, p. 119.

a lot does not necessarily increase happiness or relationship success – a quick look at celebrity relationships demonstrates this. It's clear that both of the criteria many people use to make initial date assessments (physical attractiveness and resources) have shortcomings.

Traits worth considering

It is a good idea to include in our assessments of potential life partners the traits they have. Traits are usually stable over a lifetime: extroversion, introversion, nice, mean, calm, or agitated, for example. Are our potential life partners emotionally available, open or closed? Do they have common sense? What are their values and interests? What are their families like and how do they act and behave with them? These are all telling traits that might well be worth taking into account when choosing someone as a life partner. It is unlikely these traits will be visible in the early dating stages of a relationship as we strive to make the person see only the best version of ourselves. Therefore it is only after having engaged with someone that we come to know better how well matched we might be.

Same-sex couples report similar physical attraction desires to those reported by heterosexual couples, but they do appear to be less caught up in career and to be more into connectedness. Anna (early 30s) said that she finally went to a meet-up group (organised online) to find a partner and, 'I remember the absolute terror of going to this, but I made brilliant friends.' She met her current partner of two years there, and the relationship grew slowly. It is characterised by 'being able to be myself. It is easy, normal and I can assume support.'

Tom (28) says that his relationship was not based on instant attraction, and he was already in another relationship when he met his current partner. 'Within three weeks we knew we meant something to each other,' he explains, but it was the texting that put substance into the relationship: 'We texted hundreds of texts every day and we realised we liked each other.'

Texting and attraction

Texting can be a way of increasing attraction, and it can be an instance in which technology becomes an aid to romance. Getting and sending texts during the day while carrying on a normal life can be everything from caring and cute to sexy. It can keep a relationship alive while distance or work get in the way. A couple of words can warm the heart and remind partners of their attraction to each other. Ben (35) says that he uses 'text conversations more than speaking' at the early stages of a relationship. 'When I meet a woman, the next step is texting, as to call or speak would be a bit too forward.'

The *Enduring Love* survey in the UK found that couples used texting to negotiate practicalities, practise intimacy, express emotional closeness and mediate the relationship. As one researcher explains: 'In some cases, texting was felt to be a safer and less intrusive way to communicate than through phone conversations or face to face.'[8] When face-

---

8   Singh, R., 'Enduring Love? Couple Relationships in the 21st Century. Clinical Implications. Feedback', *Journal of the Family Therapy Association of Ireland*, Summer 2015, p. 74.

to-face conversations might lead to arguments, some couples even Skype from one room to another as an aid to having a better conversation.

This use of technology as a mediator of relationships may increase as the population of technology-savvy young people become involved with each other. They are comfortable with technology and have experience of being intimate online; they may find that it helps rather than hinders conversation. However, there is a danger with the immediacy of texting. For example, texting at 2 a.m. when feeling angry and vulnerable might cause unnecessary angst in the relationship. A general rule that might help would be to decide never to text after 10 p.m. or before 8 a.m. – this might allow consciousness and reasonableness to function better. If you need to discuss something important, doing it in person will create many more possibilities for resolution.

Repeating mistakes

It is often the case that people find they are always attracted to the same type of person; even when they want to change this, they find it very difficult. If you are always attracted to an outgoing, charismatic and charming mate, but your experience tells you that they never commit, then it is important to try to develop an attraction for someone more stable. This is easier said than done! You may find that you are bored by the lack of challenge and are uncomfortable with certainty, but it is worth persevering with this.

Our family backgrounds can also come into play here. You may, for example, have a high level of tolerance for emotional distance, or ways other than those in which your family demonstrated love and affection. Conversely, you may want to repeat your family's principles and consciously seek those in a partner. Amy (32) recognises the heritage she has received from her family: 'Coming from my family, who have worked hard, I am always attracted to hard-working guys.' One of her ways of judging a guy is to ask herself, 'What would my cousins or family think of him?' We need self-awareness so that we are choosing consciously for ourselves – we may want to repeat our family patterns or do the exact opposite – but this decision will need awareness if we are to exercise choice.

Changing to what is good for us

Some effort and work needs to go into developing what is truly good for us. If you know a certain type of person is not going to be good for you, then giving in to this attraction on an ongoing basis is predictable and unintelligent. If possible, date people you admire and who inspire you, rather than following raw physical attraction. While it might be less thrilling initially, it will begin to make you feel more confident, and you can begin a relationship that has a more solid basis. If we come from a background where love was demonstrated with loudness and cynicism, we may find that we are bored initially with commitment and quietness. These will take some time to get used to, but they may be worth investigating as they may be exactly what our lives need.

Getting into a relationship requires most people to step outside their comfort zone and put themselves in the way of meeting other single people. These days, this happens mostly online. It needs courage, perseverance and intelligence, but these are qualities worth growing for life anyway. To maximise your own level of attraction, simply be healthier, like being yourself, and practise confidence by focusing attention away from yourself and on what is interesting about the other person. Resilience is also required, in the form of not taking rejections personally: understand that we cannot understand others' motives until we know them better. If the date hasn't worked out, it is best to let it go; the most successful way of doing this is to re-engage with the dating game and find someone else who is interesting to meet. The very fact of engaging or re-engaging with dating will stretch and develop you; with perseverance, the possibility of success increases.

Be careful what you practise

It is a phenomenon that people in their twenties can spend a decade or more in a relationship with the view that it will do while they wait for something better to come along. This is a very dangerous thing to do: neither person sees the other as their first choice and both are practising 'putting up with'. This has detrimental results. Sometimes neither of them meets the person of their dreams, and then they become angry and frustrated at their partners for causing them to miss out on their opportunities. Another outcome is that, as the years pass, it becomes impossible to leave or commit as the couple become good at tolerating an 'okay' situation. It is arguably better to split up and, if it seems right, to choose each other again fully and properly at a later time when it is right to settle down. Fear of being alone or fear of being seen to be single is often the driving factor. However, no one wants fear to run their lives! Make a decision, take action and follow through on plans for your future – even if it means suffering some loneliness. Acting with faith in yourself will attract others to you and open up possibilities.

Assuming that the initial stages of dating have been successfully negotiated, then the next stage of settling into the relationship can begin.

4

Beginnings of relationships

Many couples say that the beginning of a relationship is the most blissful time in their lives. It is a period people refer back to as 'the glory days'. However, many cannot seem to move the relationship beyond this stage. The relationship can become fraught with the problems of long-distance separation, or the outcome may be not commitment but perpetual 'flatmatedom' (where a couple live like flatmates, sharing the costs, without ever taking on the title or responsibilities of boyfriend/girlfriend).

The biological clock often ticks loudly, but so does the career clock; often, the start of the relationship happens when work is expanding and the demands of life, career and the relationship may feel like too much stress. The start of the relationship is also a time when couples form habits and rituals – often without consciously doing so – and these lay down a framework for the future relationship. Exercising awareness and effort at this time can have lifelong benefits and can ensure that future unhappiness is diverted.

Being in love creates an openness in us that often makes us better versions of ourselves. It is like enjoying a better 'me', and we often think this will last forever – but in fact it is similar to a gift that has to be earned. If you want to maintain the more generous, kind, light-hearted, affectionate you that the initial stages of love have created, then you have to do the hard work to ensure that this is long-lasting. For example, imagine a person who is witty, active and communicative in the early stages of a relationship, but who retreats back into a non-communicative, passive self after the first year or eighteen months. There is an opportunity in the first months to experience what it is like to be stretched and developed, and to avoid later retreating into an earlier version of yourself. The time to make that development a constant is when it is easy – when you are in love.

Creating new habits and patterns can be as hard as letting go of the old ones, and, of course, this can only happen if you are aware of your habits. This means that if you want to create a new habit – such as being more considerate or empathetic – you would have to practise it on a daily basis, with feedback and reinforcement for a considerable time, before you could assess whether it has established a hold or not. The previous chapter explained that being healthy, confident and resilient are all very attractive qualities. Letting go of rejection and self-criticism also contribute to the development of both self and the relationship. This letting go is all about not taking things personally, but instead acknowledging that the other person has a right to say yes or no too – we need to accept this fully without rumination and endless analysis.

The ideal time to look at these development issues is when you are already outside your usual sense of self-protection (i.e. when you are in love) and you have a partner who totally believes in your capacity to be fantastic.

Creating healthy couple habits

Consciously deciding to lead a healthy life as a couple and as an individual will set a pattern for the future: if you love sitting on the couch, drinking wine and watching Netflix, you will need to balance it with hikes, sport, dancing or yoga, or some other form of exercise that you both enjoy. While we often have difficulty getting ourselves to do things that are good for us, it is easy to be enthusiastic about our partner's well-being; this can make developing good habits of exercise and getting fresh air more painless at the beginning of a relationship, as you promote health in your loved one. However, the early stages of coupledom often include dining out, late-night chips and celebratory drinks, and we can seem like killjoys when considering healthy eating and exercise at this time. But these habits can be killers to change later, when their effects take hold, so it is important to try. Because of the huge influence that couples have on each other at this early stage, it will only take one person to be committed to exercise and nutrition for the change to begin. Obviously we need to take our partner's preferences into account, as insisting they go to tae kwon do may not be their idea of fun. Remember, healthy people are very attractive, and we all want our partner to find us attractive as we age; this is worth keeping in mind as we try to establish good patterns.

Technological habits have infiltrated today's relationships. It is now common to see couples sitting on the couch, TV on and two laptops and smartphones at the ready. It can feel as though there are dozens of people in the relationship and the possibility for intimacy decreases. One half of the couple can be connected deeply to someone in another country, while the other is struggling to get a look-in. Some discussion on this is necessary at an early stage, so that the couple prioritises actual over virtual conversation. Such a discussion can put some guidelines in place, such as no technology in the bedroom or at mealtimes. It is strange that we can feel lonely with our partners in the same room, but the intimacy of the virtual world can mean that if we are engaged in it we are totally unavailable to the people right beside us. Awareness of this is crucial.

Letting go of negative thoughts

One of the easiest ways of becoming more confident is to let go of endless, familiar and persistent negative thoughts that tell you that you are worthless or not good enough. It is worthwhile doing something about these self-criticisms.

Having a partner whom you can't get enough of is very helpful in assisting with this project. When we have negative thoughts, there is always an accompanying tension in the body (often in the form of tightness in the stomach, chest or head), and becoming aware of this is the first step towards freedom. Giving attention to your partner instead of focusing on the thoughts immediately gives relief. Often, the more physical the attention the better; kissing, hugging, tickling, pinching or sniffing will all break the thought process and stop the incessant feeding of the negativity.

Again, the early stages of a relationship in which you are adored and affirmed is the time when you are most likely to be successful in challenging anti-confidence and negative thinking, so any effort you put in at this time is likely to be more successful. Now is the time to start training the mind to focus on the present and not on endless thinking. There are many books, courses and podcasts that can help in this process.

Insecurity and fear of rejection

Another trait worth engaging with at the beginning of a relationship is insecurity or fear of rejection. This fear can be crippling and can lead to clinginess or a constant requirement for affirmation that might eventually confirm anxiety, as the partner has to get away from the suffocation of a too-close relationship. The problem with finding happiness is often the immediate fear of losing it, and this can result in holding on too tight.

The truth is that we cannot force people to stay unless they choose to, and if we live in fear we are more likely to drive them away. Give your partner the freedom to be with you (or not) and keep your judgement open and intelligent, so that you are responding to what is real and not to what is imagined in the relationship. All relationships have trajectories; the best approach is to stay where the relationship is, and not where you think it should be or might be.

It can happen that the mind travels faster than the experience, and we might be looking at marriage and commitment when in fact the relationship is only in its infancy. This leads to expectations and decisions that are not appropriate, and panic can set in. Learning to breathe and manage panic, accepting yourself completely, and not hiding or feeding your fears are all practices with lifelong benefits. It can be difficult not to anticipate what is to come, but this inevitably leads to inappropriate thoughts and actions. Staying in the present and trusting yourself to meet what today brings will lead to better responses and more confidence. Being present is simply a matter of connecting your mind to your body in this moment – breathing and focusing on touch or sound or sight will instantly offer grounding.

Exit-strategy partners and fear of commitment

The opposite of clingy people are people who are ready to bolt at the first sign that a relationship might be for the long term. They may have a fear of being trapped or may have had negative past experiences or, indeed, may be carrying a torch for a previous lover. These are all their personal issues that they need to address (through reflection or perhaps counselling), but the issues will have a big effect on the relationship. If we challenge people in this category too soon, there is no doubt that the relationship will end; however, if we don't challenge them at all, there is the danger that an ending is inevitable, and we can waste time in the false belief that commitment is in the offing. The person who has a fear of commitment needs to feel safe and unpressured, but the issue also needs to be a topic of conversation – again, the timing of this is crucial. If we do it too soon, before the relationship has any basis, then the exit is assured; if we leave it too late, there is the danger of regret and anger at the lost time.

Often the biological clock has a way of forcing this

conversation; this is a reality for women and one that deserves attention. There is a need for good judgement here, and you can gather this from others as well as the potential partner. Are there people in this person's family and friendship circle who are married and happy? What is the relationship history and is there any evidence of commitment? If you met online, what did his or her profile say that he or she was looking for? A casual relationship? Then it is important to take that person at his or her word and disentangle yourself before you are very hurt.

However, some people just need experience and time in a good relationship to come to the discussion of commitment, and you have to make the decision of what the current situation is. Ty Tashiro proposes that 'the signs of a relationship's disastrous future are evident before individuals fall madly in love, painted in vibrant colours of their problematic traits'.[1] If a person is emotionally distant, struggles with maintaining contact, or is unreliable, then we need to take these into account when we consider a long-term relationship with this person. Because falling in love blocks our capacity for rationality, it might be important to check with family and friends what they see as the possibility for an enduring relationship, before deciding to stay and weather the challenge of the exit-focused partner.

Maintaining friendship groups

With the lure and intensity of the loved-up relationship,

---

1 Tashiro (2014), p. 83.

it can be very easy to let friendship groups slide. There is a huge cost to this: friends will feel the rejection and not, perhaps, be willing to come back and support you when the relationship takes a dip or ends. Eric (25) says that when his girlfriend 'dumped' him suddenly, he was broken, but his best friend stayed over with him for a long time until he was back on his feet again. This is when friendship comes into its own – when someone will bear witness to your pain and stand beside you while you suffer.

There is also the danger that the romantic relationship becomes the repository for all the emotional and security needs that a couple has; it is unlikely that the relationship can or will meet all these requirements. The beginning of a relationship is a time when you need good friendships, so that the relationship is not creaking under the weight of every emotional need. Think of the devastation when a break-up happens and the only person you have any experience of speaking to of such intimate things is the partner who is doing the rejecting. The isolation resulting from this exclusive intimacy can be dangerous, and the main antidote is to maintain friendships right through the romantic relationship. Friends will also offer you some objectivity if you need to question the relationship or any aspect of it, and they may also spot traits that you do not notice in the throes of romance. Keeping up social times with your friends needs to be a strong component of early romantic life; these dates with friends need to be sacrosanct and not subject to change when your new partner wants to do something nice together. The loyalty you show friends will be evidence of the same loyalty you will demonstrate later as the relationship progresses.

Long-distance relationships

'Without you is doing time,' sang Sonny Condell at a recent concert by the band Scullion in Dublin; yet the long-distance relationship is now very much a norm, as couples work in different cities – or even countries.[2] Most people warn against it, however, as it can be extremely difficult to maintain. Long-distance relationships often happen when one partner gets a job in another country. Indeed, one partner may be *from* another country, which can add to the difficulty. Almost everyone interviewed had experienced a long-distance relationship at some stage. Some couples had managed to live successfully with this; usually their success was due to both agreeing that their career demanded this situation. Jake and Loren said, 'We both made a decision to concentrate on work, and we have put no time limit on it.' Loren said that she was 'close to burn out' as she works full throttle when Jake is not there. They have very supportive families who understand their ambition, and Skype has allowed them to participate in each other's lives. They are very conscious of the possibility of rows when they meet, due to the build-up of expectation; however, they are very careful not to take out their frustration on each other, and they recognise they need 'assimilation time'.

Clodagh (living in New York) says that long distance is

---

2   Condell, S., Whelans, Dublin, 22 August 2015.

an 'excellent test of the relationship: if you can put up with it, you have thought about it a lot'. However, she adds that such a relationship is very likely to break up, as it is 'so difficult'. Many interviewees agreed that fidelity in long-distance relationships should be assumed in the same manner as in same-country relationships; however, talking about this is important, as temptation and opportunity are constant issues. Amy says, 'Long distance is a tough way of doing things, and I would not do it again readily.' Josh and his wife have created a family life that has long distance at its core, but there have been moments when its dangers have been very evident: 'Once there was an earthquake when the two of us were away, and we felt very guilty about the children.' Josh says that they have tried all methods of communication but 'writing can be a great way of shedding emotion'. Writing is not as immediate as Skype, but it allows some reflection and thought to go into the communication.

If long distance is part of the relationship from the very beginning, there will be adjustments to make and all assumptions will have to be dissected, so that communication can be close and intimate. Text, email, Skype and FaceTime all facilitate this, but the couple will need to be clear that they are on a relationship trajectory in the same way as others, and they'll need to create milestones and meet them. There is a temptation either to move too fast in the relationship, creating a false intimacy, or perhaps to let the dating situation go on too long; constant and real communication is the key in this situation.

The early stages of a relationship can be a very special time when love is at the forefront and is expressed in a myriad of ways. However, these stages also include the creation of dreams and hopes. Many couples become stressed by finances when they look at buying a house together, and all that this entails. If they allow stress to dominate at this time, the future for a stress-free life looks bleak. The aim should be to enjoy and wallow in the love, expansion and personal development that this time allows. If the couple can become adept at enjoyment and connection during these years, the chances increase of these being part of their whole time together.

5

What to do and not to do

Marriage (or a long-term relationship) can actually be good for you. Not only does it boost physical health in men and mental well-being in women, but the longer it endures, the greater are the benefits, resulting in a longer and more satisfying life. According to a 2011 newspaper article:

> Traditionally, people thought it was a good idea and nearly everyone was married, it was hard to make a comparison. But over the last thirty years there has been a lot more social diversity so we are able to make these evaluations. The bottom line is that medically speaking, the group with the greatest longevity are the marrieds.[1]

David and John Gallacher conducted a study involving millions of people over many years across seven European countries; they concluded that married people have mortality rates ten to fifteen per cent lower than the population as a whole, and they argue that well-adjusted individuals are more likely to establish long-term relationships. They suggest that the determining factor may not be marriage itself, but the kind of people likely to wed and stay wed.[2] People

---

1 Dr Gallacher, quoted in the *Evening Herald*, 28 January 2011, p. 28.
2 Gallacher, D. and Gallacher, J., 'Are Relationships Good for Your

who have managed to stay with a partner for many years have probably developed capacities and skills that have stretched their partners as people; however, there is always the possibility that they have mainly practised stubbornness and refusal!

Marriage remains very popular, in spite of increasing rates of divorce and separation and a rising sense of cynicism. Gay and lesbian couples have achieved the right to what the great majority of other couples want: 'a social recognition in marriage of their personal achievement and effort'.[3] Maureen Gaffney argues that the priority for couples is establishing a close and intimate relationship, characterised by open communication and a strong commitment to negotiate important issues: 'added to the expectation of love and friendship is the hope that the relationship will help both partners to express their innermost, deepest feelings, each helping the other to be his or her best self'.[4]

Long-term relationships, involving commitment, would seem to be a pinnacle of human achievement and having one may be the aim of many people. But no training for such relationships is available (other than short pre-marriage courses – for example those required/offered by some churches). Many couples operate from assumptions and myths about what makes a relationship work. John Gottman, however, conducted research throughout the 1980s and

---

Health?', *Student British Medical Journal* (2011), http://www.medscape.com/viewarticle/739824_1 (accessed 16 May 2016).

3 Gaffney, M., 'Marriage Just Isn't What it Used to Be', *The Irish Times*, 28 March 2015, p. 4.

4 *Ibid.*

1990s on more than 3,000 couples in a specially outfitted studio apartment in Seattle that was nicknamed the 'Love Lab'. These two decades of research have led to ongoing studies all verifying the same data. Gottman found that he could predict separation with ninety-one per cent accuracy, simply by analysing variables in a couple's behaviour during a five-minute disagreement.[5]

So what can we learn from the studies in the Love Lab? What can we do to make a long-term relationship last and what should we avoid doing? What does research by Gottman and others tell us?

Resolving conflict

Gottman found that most couples fought. What was interesting was that even the most happily married couples never resolved sixty-nine per cent of their conflicts. Gottman discovered that fighting was not the cause of breaking-up; rather, *how* couples fought was the determining factor. Gottman extracted what he called the 'Four Horsemen of the Apocalypse' to describe the four factors present in an argument that are most likely to lead to divorce. In *The Seven Principles for Making Marriage Work*, Gottman and Silver outline these in detail.[6] They are all very common:

1. *Criticism.* Criticism is the most divisive factor in a relationship; it can be completely silent, but the effect is

---

5   Butler, K., 'The Art & Science of Love', *Psychotherapy Networker*, Sept/ Oct 2006, p. 30.
6   Gottman, J. and Silver, N., *The Seven Principles for Making Marriage Work* (Orion, London, 2007).

always a direct hit. It suggests that the person is essentially not good in some way. It is not aimed at behaviour but at something more personal and deep. Because it is often not voiced or it is only hinted at, it can be proffered without anyone taking direct responsibility for it. Think of the tone in which 'Nice of you to come home' can be spoken, and the subtlety of criticism is clear. The main effect is one of isolation or intimidation, so it is likely that criticism has been given if a person is feeling either of these things.

2. *Contempt.* Contempt can come in the form of sneering, eye-rolling or turning away when the other partner is speaking. It is very dismissive and often takes the form of name-calling either to the person's face or behind the person's back. Think of the effect of saying 'She is just useless' or 'He is a waste of space', whether that is said directly or to a friend. Sarcasm and cynicism are all types of contempt, and Gottman and Silver say, 'It is poisonous to a relationship because it conveys disgust.'[7]

3. *Defensiveness.* Interestingly, research reveals that defensiveness is more problematic than nagging or blaming. When we are attacked, we often challenge it by denying responsibility and pointing out that, actually, we 'emptied the dishwasher only last week'. This rarely has the desired effect of getting the other person to see our worthiness; instead, the conflict is escalated by the subtle implication of blaming the partner for the escalating situation.

---

7   *Ibid.,* p. 29.

4. *Stonewalling*. Stonewalling happens when one person is so overwhelmed by the conflict that he or she tunes out the other person, going through the motions of being there but actually being emotionally and mentally unavailable. This is a defence mechanism and is perhaps understandable at times, but it is impossible to have a relationship when one person has departed in all but physical form.

It is likely that most couples have engaged in arguing using these four factors, but it is unlikely that couples have been aware of just how destructive they are. The presence of the 'Four Horsemen' alone, Gottman found – combined with pulse rates that rose above ninety-five beats per minute during a disagreement – were highly reliable predictors of divorce. However, there is an answer: he found that there is a five-to-one ratio in that successful couples 'made at least five positive remarks or gestures toward each other for every zinger during a fight', and for these couples in calmer times their positive-to-negative ratio was an astounding twenty-to-one.[8]

Mary (twenty-five years married), in answer to the question of what makes marriage work, says: 'For me it is to learn how to fight in the context of a committed relationship and to know and agree that fighting is not the end, or a bad sign but can be often the way through and forward.'

---

8 Butler (2006), p. 30.

Five-to-one ratio

A five-to-one ratio of affection, personal joy and humour in arguments is something to aim for (that is five remarks showing affection, personal joy or humour for every negative remark in an argument):

- *Affection* is a hugely positive way to rebalance the argument. Learning how to argue with affection, and a sense that someone will always have your back, is key. Commitment allows the fight to happen in a way that does not signal the end; if that is strongly established, fighting can happen without fear of separation. As Julie Schwartz Gottman says, 'Commitment means a lifetime promise of devotion and care. Where there's commitment, there's no worry of being replaced if someone "better" comes along.'[9] Ted (fourteen years with his partner) explains: 'Once one's idea of commitment becomes weakened, it takes very little to begin to erode an otherwise sturdy relationship. I once heard a wise person say, "Love is more a question of the will than the fluttering of the heart." If we let our sense of commitment depend upon what we are feeling at any given moment, I feel there is almost no chance that the relationship can go the distance. Commitment underlies feelings and anchors the relationship.'

- *Humour* is also key. If we could lighten up and not take everything so seriously, we would perhaps have better

---

9   Gottman and Schwartz Gottman, (Nov/Dec 2015), p. 53.

arguments. Remember that sixty-nine per cent of arguments will never be resolved and resolution is not necessary for a successful relationship. Gerry (thirty-one years with his partner) says: 'Always maintain a sense of humour. Never forget it was you that chose him or her and remember why.' A good idea is to put a reminder that says 'lighten up' on your mobile phone. The chances are that every time you see the memo, you *will* lighten up. We can be very serious about our lives, and usually when we look back on that time we can question whether it was worth all the worry.

- *Personal joy* is crucial in learning how to create the five-to-one ratio. If we invest in liking ourselves, we will not be easily dismissed; instead, we will be able to hold our own truth, even if our partner does not agree. Shouting someone down does not win an argument; a confident person can have the patience to wait for another opportunity to resolve the difficulty.

The 'good argument': making fighting productive

We argue with our loved ones because it matters to us that they understand where we are coming from. However, common responses to conflict are avoidance or agreeing for the sake of peace, and these strategies can lead to problems for both sides. The person doing the avoiding is never heard, so their confidence goes down and their partner never actually understands their point of view. 'Anything for peace' is a quick and easy way out of a potential conflict, but the cost is an unwillingness to engage with the person with whom you are spending your life. It is an honour if someone takes the time to engage with you to find out your position, especially if he or she holds an opposing idea. Fighting or disagreeing is a very intimate activity; it can be productive if you do it in a way that takes both perspectives on board and is open to a new outcome.

The following are some ideas about how to assist in the 'good argument':

- Always start with 'no matter what happens, I will always have your back', and then speak honestly.

- Agree to have a hug at the end of an argument and agree that this happens regardless of feeling – that is even if feeling angry or resentful, engage in the hug for a minute.

- Have arguments only in specific places. This will allow for some special, protected places in your life, such as bedrooms or living rooms.

- If things get very heated and there is no listening, agree to go away for twenty minutes and then come back; both people will be calmer and more reasonable. The trick is to come back!

- Avoidance is not a good method to resolve an argument; the argument usually surfaces again in another form at a later time.

- Breathe, pause and do not assume you know what is

going on in your partner's head. As Padraig O'Morain notes, 'We lead somewhat pushed and driven lives at the moment, but the quality of our lives can be improved by cultivating the art of the pause.'[10]

- Remember, we fight only if we care about something. Do your partner the honour of listening to what they have to say before you disagree with him or her.

Michael (twenty-eight years married) says:

We've both got to agree in explicit language that each will give ground somewhere in meals, expectations, sex, use of the cupboard upstairs in the study, use of the current account with the extra money in it, how he will treat her boring relatives, etc., etc. Whatever it is. And here's the key: that explicit agreement will need to be rediscussed and agreed over and over again in clear language terms understood by both.

Communication

Women are usually the partners who bring up difficult issues or unhappiness in relationships. In order for women to be happy and emotionally functioning, they need a good relationship. Gottman and Silver explain: 'More than 80% of the time it is the wife who brings up sticky marital issues, while the husband tries to avoid discussing them. This isn't a symptom of a troubled marriage – it's true in most happy

---

10 O'Morain, P., 'That's Men: Relationships, like Artichokes, require Pause for Thought', *The Irish Times*, 7 July 2015, p. 13.

marriages as well.'[11] Communication seems to be the key, and in the *Enduring Love* survey most participants agreed that this is so. Making time to listen and talk is highly valued; it is a means through which couples come to understand, reassure and comfort each other. Getting along and 'having a laugh' together alleviates – or puts into perspective – the everyday strains and difficulties of life.[12]

Women also experience partners' unwillingness and/or inability to express their feelings as adversely impacting the emotional dynamics of the relationship. Often, it is in the middle of conflict that people express most emotion, and this can become a pattern of intimacy that ultimately is destructive for the relationship. Intense disagreement or fighting can often be a substitute for intimacy, and this does not bode well for the relationship.

We often need to train ourselves to have honest, intimate and real conversations, and many couples benefit from creating a structure around this. One such structure is a twenty-minute exchange during which one partner asks only questions about a chosen topic (perhaps about the family upbringing of the other) and the other person answers. Then another twenty minutes is put aside another time to allow the other partner to answer questions. This allows interesting or difficult things to be heard without comment or criticism. There need be no resolution, as the couple can broach the topic again the next time the twenty minutes is agreed. This creates real listening and disrupts the usual habitual rows

---

11 Gottman and Silver (2007), p. 115.
12 Gabb *et al.* (2013), p. 7.

that can happen (see *Exercise 9: Twenty-minute question-and-listening*).

Honesty creates intimacy and trust. However, honesty can be difficult, as we often lie to have an easier life or to let ourselves off the hook. This can be almost unseen, in that we might not be conscious of the effect it is having: distance and mistrust. Lydia (40s) has learned from many relationships that truth and communication are vital:

> Now I have no problem in saying things as they are. I think a relationship will get through tough times if there is compassion and understanding for the other person. Talking and keeping things out in the open leaves little room for insecurities and lack of trust. Trust takes time; playing games – particularly mind games – kills trust. Awareness teaches us to know and trust ourselves. We then instinctively, I believe, know if someone is not being honest or truthful.

However, Gottman and Silver warn that communication skills will not save a relationship, as most couples who have maintained happy marriages rarely do anything that even resembles active listening when they are upset.[13] We all know instinctively that this is true, as our emotions are so heightened in a row; however, if there is a possibility to make and receive what Gottman calls 'repair attempts', then the relationship can focus on what works. A repair attempt occurs when a person offers to put a break on things or slow

---

13 Gottman and Silver (2007), p. 11.

them down, so that the partner can feel the effort of the other person and accept it. During an argument, this might take the form of a question such as 'Are you able for this?' or 'Do you need a break?' It might be a gesture of affection or an offer of tea. Small moments like this can have a huge effect on the conflict and highlight that there is genuine care for the other behind the disagreement. When we are shouting or arguing, what we want most is for our partner to hear and understand us; if we really want this to happen, we can follow the rules of engagement as outlined above. Mostly, we get the opposite of what we are looking for when arguing; we feel dismissed and then blame the other person for not making the effort to listen. As always, self-awareness is the starting point for progress.

Many of the interviewees said the difference in a successful relationship as compared to an unsuccessful one is a change in themselves. Anna, now in a two-year same-sex relationship, explains, 'The main difference is in me. I have found depth in myself that I didn't know was there.' Lydia agrees: 'Before getting involved with anyone now I look "inside" myself before I look "outside" at the world and the person in front of me.'

In the *Enduring Love* survey, lesbian, gay, bisexual or transgendered (LGBT) participants were found to be generally more positive and happier than heterosexual participants were with the quality of their relationship and with the connection they have with their partner.[14] It is interesting to

---

14 Gabb *et al.* (2013), p. 3.

note that parents appear to be less involved in relationship building than childless couples, and that 'heterosexual parents are the group least likely to be there for each other, to make "couple time"; to pursue shared interests, to say "I love you" and to talk openly to one another.'[15] The cost to these parents is that they can lose the couple connection and find that they are estranged from each other when their children leave home; they have to figure out at that late stage if they are still compatible. Speaking and thinking of yourself as a lover as well as a parent will remind you of your relationship, but actions that define you and your partner as a couple are crucial if you are to avoid disaffection.

Tom says that the reason he is willing to go through all the difficult things that happen in a relationship is that his partner 'is my favourite thing in the world'. The *Enduring Love* survey found that the determination to think reflexively was particularly marked in accounts by lesbian and gay couples and by those who had had previous long-term relationships.[16] Again, that capacity to be aware and reflect on previous experience and exercise a determination not to repeat past mistakes is key to creating a good relationship.

Lydia says:

It took me years of repeating the same patterns of behaviour and dating before it dawned on me what I was doing and still have a tendency to do, if I don't pause and take stock, sometimes very quickly ... repeating the same behaviours over and

---

15 *Ibid.*, p. 7.
16 *Ibid.*, p. 8.

over again, expecting a different result, which is definitely in-sanity.

Impact of family of origin

Self-awareness must extend to looking at our own upbring-ing, as we may unconsciously repeat behaviours from our families or have reactions to our current partners similar to those we had as a child. All this can lead to confusion and, at worst, to rejection and ultimately separation.

Tom says, 'I see patterns in our relationship with both of us having long-suffering mothers and absent fathers. I see my mother-in-law in him, as in questioning: "Did he pick me because I heightened the emotionality that his Mum would have?"' Tom is now looking at the bigger picture and taking into account his partner's family of origin when he looks at his relationship. This is allowing him to decipher what patterns need to be addressed.

It is very helpful for a couple to have discussions about the families they grew up in, as these can bring attitudes, approaches and fears to the surface – there they can be dealt with, changed or challenged. What can otherwise happen is that the couple ends up dealing with a surface problem, while the real issue lies dormant. This results in frustration and endless repeated attempts at resolution.

Lydia very insightfully comments:

My parents split up when I was ten and got back together when I was sixteen, and I said to myself when I was little that I would never depend on a man in case he would leave me.

Yet I was looking for what I saw my father to be: a powerful man with charisma and charm, yet who was not available to me emotionally or physically for a number of years.

Even if we are aware of our family's legacy, it is often very difficult to change it. We may have a comfort zone with, for example, no affection, and may find that we have an endurance for this; we may indeed find it difficult to handle a partner who is constantly affectionate. Many couples find that the longer they are together, the more they can see the family heritage coming out; this can be disconcerting, but if it is a continuous topic for consideration it can be amusing and funny, rather than daunting. There is no doubt that if we do not want to repeat family patterns, we might have to practise a lot of self-examination, together with behaviour modification. All change and development happens outside our comfort zones, and the motivation of a better, closer relationship is very alluring. This is why the possibility for change to happen is at its highest in a relationship. Self-awareness, discussion and self-discipline are key.

Paul (in a ten-year partnership) says:

Virgil reputedly wrote 'omnia vincit amor' (love conquers all). For sure. It also surely has helped me to bear in mind that love is a decision as often as it is a feeling (usually not at the same time). And that decision for me involves the work of knowing and dissolving the stories I weave around and about myself, an clear a space for another in my heart. Then I can ly welcome them in there as an equal.

Stressors in relationships

In Chapter 2 it was noted that the *Enduring Love* survey found two of the aspects of relationships many participants least liked were poor communication and arguments, especially around money issues. For most people, their partner is also their best friend, in that they tell their partner everything and get support from them. Anxieties can arise from trying to manage household finances and perhaps not knowing about a partner's financial situation. But other stressors also often come in the form of external factors such as financial uncertainties, bereavement, ill health, the birth of children or changes in employment and housing. All of these, and other things, can pose a threat to the relationship; conversely, however, facing threats together can often bring couples closer.

Lack of money

Lack of money can make it difficult for couples who are apart to see each other. Conversely, it can also mean that couples in low-income households do not get enough time apart: lack of finances means that there is no spare money for socialising, so the couple spend all their time together at home, and this can lead to claustrophobia in the relationship.

As money symbolises power, it is important that both people have complete knowledge of and access to all the financial information. Compassion for each other around the hardship that lack of money causes is also a balm in tough times. Louise and George had taken out huge loans in the years before the financial crisis of 2008 and the recession that followed, and they found they constantly fought wi each other over who was to blame. Huge resentment meant that they could not comfort each other, and they found the lifestyle change for the children very difficult. Eventually they sought help and are now beginning to see a future for themselves as a couple.

Housework

Housework and the sharing of chores are always contentious issues, but often rows about housework serve to cover over more important issues, such as 'How do I know you have me as number one in your life?' It is often the issue of fairness − as Chapter 2 mentioned − that is at play here. Couples need open discussion of this, and also a trial-and-error approach. If someone in the house is taking over a chore (for example the laundry), he or she will need direction and support for at least a month before being competent at it. Optimism, patience and perseverance are all necessary to create fairness and change in this area of living together − it is a good idea to leave criticism, comment and sneering out of it if there is to be any possibility of success.

Paul (60), who was taking early retirement, suggested that his wife's domain was the house and he intended not to interfere with this; however, he had very strong thoughts that his adult children should do their share of the housework. When the injustice of this was pointed out to him, he good-epted that he needed to pitch in.

ither a very supportive or an irritating force in

a couple's relationship. What is important is always to respect the other person's family, and not to resort to deriding them, especially in public. It is unfair to put a partner in a 'them or me' situation; instead, aim to demonstrate unity in the relationship while allowing the partner his or her own relationship with the in-law family. There are many occasions when conflict arises, perhaps due to childcare or grandparent issues. To resolve this conflict, couples need discussion and, occasionally, outside help, before reacting or responding. Families are for life; we need to treat them with delicacy, so exercising a couple of moments' pause before coming to a conclusion is a good idea.

It may seem strange, but competition between a parent and a son/daughter-in-law can emerge as a destructive force. If the couple does not deal with it, it can grow into a lifelong battle. Some level of acceptance and benevolence is necessary. If practised, these might free up the in-law so that he or she is much less affected by the situation and thus more open to possibilities for connection.

Sex and intimacy

Sex and intimacy are often contentious in relationships. The next chapter will cover these subjects.

Sharing interests versus distance

One person speaking for a couple (thirty-five years married) said:

> G and I talked and we both agreed that a huge help for us was having shared interests, especially playing sport together

and with friends. Also planning rewards for our hard work, e.g. holidays. My experience with people with relationship problems taught me that partners are often trying to guess what the other wants (often wrongly) instead of simply asking – this way they get the correct answer!

'Opposites attract' goes an old saying, but in fact 'similarities attract' is a better guide for much relationship success; sharing meaning in life and having areas of common ground and interest make for great companionship. It can happen that when couples get married or commit to each other, they then focus completely on other things (work, golf or drama groups, for example). Very quickly, the sense that the other person is a life companion can disappear, so it is important to have things in common, to share rich experiences and have contact that binds. In this scenario, it is easy to assume that one person knows what the other is thinking or going to say or do, and this can create silences or boredom. We should always enquire about, always be interested in, the thoughts and ideas of the other. This will keep the relationship from being too settled.

However, relationships need a sense of mystery, and we can easily create this if it *is* a case of 'opposites attract'. In this situation, there is always interest, because it is not possible for one person to assume what the other is thinking. Lack of communication can cause problems, however, as it becomes very difficult to gain understanding or empathy for the other person. Mystery requires some level of the unknown to keep the spark alive, but too much can result in apathy.

The 'too close' versus 'too distant' conundrum is personal to each couple, and it is necessary to negotiate it regularly. It may also have resonances in the pasts of both people, in that their parents may have had relationships where they never went out together – or went out *only* together. This is part of the ongoing play of the partnership and the couple should enjoy and confront it at regular stages.

Knowing what to do and what not to do in relationships is a matter of using research and knowledge, and mixing it with experience, reflection on the past and discussion with others about what makes things work. There are stages in relationships, and if we negotiate these with self-awareness, we can avoid some unnecessary pitfalls. These stages are often determined by external factors – for example, the birth of children, the death of parents, illness, unemployment, children leaving home, retirement or moving house. Using the wisdom and experience of others who have gone through this is intelligent and might save you some anguish. If possible, the most important aspect to carry through to the end is the commitment that you have chosen this person and he or she is, and will be, the most important person in your life. One person speaking for a couple (twenty years married) explained:

> The key to an enduring relationship: I remember years ago promising each other that, no matter what, we would always stay close. Whenever we drift we remind each other of that … I also believe that we should never stop making each other feel like the most special person alive: that way it doesn't

matter what's going on outside the two of us; if all else falls apart we still have each other.

If the relationship is going well, we don't usually look for information on what works or not. It is only when things are breaking down or becoming uncomfortable that we look for ways of addressing or fixing problems. Sometimes we wait so long that the relationship in is serious trouble before we call attention to it and the effort it takes to repair it is then monumental. There are times when we feel that we are alone in our efforts, and we can experience this as very isolating and unrewarding. However, there was something special that made us commit in the first place, and this was of enough significance that we chose to be with that person. There is a body of knowledge on relationships that can help: reading, talking to others or attending a couples counsellor will offer access to this resource. The earlier the intervention, the better the possibility of a good outcome. The person who accesses this is the one with the most awareness at that time.

6

Sex and intimacy
in relationships

Sex and intimacy in relationships are very important topics, and yet ones that people rarely discuss in any depth. The sex education we get at school is largely biological or fear-based. We then discover through various means that sex can be pleasurable and fun, and that it can create the best glue for keeping a couple together. The early stages of a relationship are often marked by a feeling of insatiability. Ronan (30) says, 'I couldn't get enough of her and I just wanted to almost eat her up.' Desire wakes us up; all our senses are alive to the world and we glory in the brilliance of living. We often try to keep this stage, or we mourn when it passes, or try to recreate it by having many start-up relationships. Our focus in this initial stage is almost totally on the other person, and we see how wonderful he or she is; in the opposite direction, being in receipt of this attention creates in us the feeling of being so special and needed that we feel invincible and powerful. Because we feel so powerful, this desire can engender in us an expansiveness and generosity towards the world; we are more compassionate and forgiving of those around us and more optimistic about our futures. Of course, all this has an aim: to create future generations for the human race and ensure our DNA survives.

If all that sounds a bit too perfect, it is. Several difficulties can arise to dim the sheen of this seeming perfection. Numerous people experience problems in their sexual relationships right from the very beginning. Many couples have good sex at the beginning of the relationship, but it peters out quickly, and they struggle to get that spark back. Others experience lack of desire, lack of orgasm or some kind of dysfunction; still others have intimacy difficulties and cannot make love to the person they have chosen. Our pasts can interfere, and the sexual messages we received at home or school can have an impact that creates blocks. Conversely, the requirement to be excellent at everything can lead to sex becoming all about performance – it becomes another task at which to excel. The influence of porn is emerging as extensive, and couples can struggle to have conversations about it. Stress, exhaustion and lack of time can all lead to sexual difficulties that cause the early connection to become a past dream. The need to have the perfect body can lead to self-absorption and criticism. The pressure of getting pregnant can cause sex to be a function rather than a pleasure. Whatever the difficulty, sex – and particularly intimacy – in a relationship is hugely important to most couples. The lack of it can lead to rows, betrayal and, sometimes, break-up.

Sex surveys can give us pointers as to the way in which many people conduct their intimate lives, but there is always the caveat that people lie or exaggerate in surveys about how well their sex lives are going. Surveys can, however, give some helpful indicators of what the norm is as we try to locate ourselves on a continuum, instead of struggling alone with our deepest anxieties. One such survey is the *Irish Times* sex survey published on 30 June 2015.[1] This survey used responses from more than 12,000 participants, two-thirds of whom were between the ages of twenty-four and fifty, and its results are indicative rather than definitive.

Use it or lose it!

In the *Irish Times* survey, almost all categories of participant said that sex was 'very important' to a committed relationship. Sixty-six per cent of heterosexual men reported 'really enjoying' sex and said that it is 'really important' in a committed relationship. Just under half of heterosexual women said that they 'really enjoyed' sex, while homosexual women were more enthusiastic about enjoying sex (sixty-eight per cent). The UK *Enduring Love* survey agrees that 'there is a consensus that sex remains an important part of a relationship', but points also to divisions in the experiences of men and women. For example, one female respondent reported that she has sex when she doesn't really want to and a male respondent said, 'We have wonderful sex very often; it makes me feel loved and cared for.'[2] The researchers conclude that childless men and women are fifty per cent more likely than parents to perceive physical affection as a sign of appreciation, and that men are three times more likely than women to mention sexual intimacy as something that makes them feel appreciated. All this shows that sex is

---

1   Holmquist, K., 'Let's Talk about Sex: The Full Survey Results', *The Irish Times*, 30 June 2015.

2   Gabb *et al.* (2013), p. 8.

part of a complex intermingling of closeness, appreciation and connection between couples. While sex can demonstrate all these things, it is also possible for couples to express closeness without any sex.

There are many points in a couple's life together when it can become more problematic to continue having sex than it is at other times. These more problematic points can be stages (such as marriage, the birth of children or menopause), but can also be linked to confidence-shattering events (such as unemployment, illness or tragedy). Habit also plays a strong role; it can have a positive effect at times of ongoing stress. For example, if a couple has always had sex on a Saturday morning, then it is possible that they will continue to do that in spite of tiredness, lack of motivation or little interest (perhaps due to exhaustion, for example from night feeds). In discussing this topic, women of middle age advised 'use it or lose it', as both the pattern of sex and the desire for it are linked to practice and routine. We can find it difficult to see sex as something routine, because we love the idea of romance and spontaneity; yet, it is often the routine that gets a couple through the difficult times. One woman, who is busy with small children, a full-time job and a night course, said that when her husband wants sex, 'I wish he hadn't heard of foreplay, because I just want to finish it and get on with the next thing I have to do.' She said this jokingly but truthfully, and yet, if they continue to have sex, she may at some time be in a position to relax and see it as something of value in itself.

In the *Irish Times* survey, almost half of all participants said that they had sex at least once a week; only fourteen per cent said that this happened three times a week. Couples in the twenty-five to thirty-four age group (the age that people are most likely to get into a relationship) are having the most sex, verifying that having a committed partner increases intimacy in the early stages of a relationship. However, the survey showed that after this age the amount of sex decreases, and how regularly people have sex falls considerably the longer people are together. The percentage of couples who have sex at least once a week drops for those who have been together for between two and seven years; it decreases further for those who have been together for between seven and fifteen years. The good news is that if the couple manages to negotiate this time (up to fifteen years), then the possibility of regular sex increases again.[3] The couples questioned, who had been together for thirty years or more, were having more regular sex. Perhaps none of this is surprising, as the demands of career, childcare, care of parents and financial pressures all push sex down the list of what is important during those frantic years. Yet we know that, for men, regular sex makes them feel appreciated, and for women, feeling desired is a very life-affirming trait.

Regular intimacy develops emotional and interpersonal awareness and sustains closeness and connections. What allows good sex to happen in a relationship are the qualities that solidify and unify a couple: trust, feeling desired and good communication. Without intimacy, it takes a lot more

---

3   Holmquist, 'Let's Talk about Sex' (2015).

effort to achieve these things, but couples can also achieve closeness with lots of physical (non-sexual) affection.

Creating opportunities for intimacy on many levels

We can create opportunities for intimacy on many levels: physically, emotionally and mentally.

Physically

We can physically create opportunities for intimacy by devising conducive circumstances, such as by introducing candles, soft lighting, music, sensual materials and privacy. For many people, a lock on the bedroom door and a music system can kick-start romantic possibilities. Alain de Botton makes a persuasive case for the use of hotel bedrooms, as the routine of normal life causes us to fail to see the erotic side of our partners:

> Hence the metaphysical importance of hotels. Their walls, beds, comfortably upholstered chairs, room-service menus, televisions and small, tightly wrapped soaps can do more than answer a taste for luxury; they can also encourage us to reconnect with our long lost sexual selves. There is no limit to what a shared dip in an alien bath may help us achieve.[4]

A trip to a hotel can reconnect us to the eroticism of our partners and reignite the sexual spark that first drew us to-

---

4   De Botton, A., *How to Think More about Sex* (Pan Macmillan, London, 2012), p. 76.

gether. Boredom and housework can be blocks to intimacy; we should take any opportunity for sex with our partners that creates playfulness, loss of control and imagination.

Candlelit dinners, moonlit walks, flowers, chocolates and good wine all have romantic associations, and we can use all of these to create a mood for love. Sometimes something edgy can be helpful to get us out of our routinised selves; this could be in the form of an adventurous activity, or sport, or a journey to an as-yet-unvisited country or place that piques our senses.

Focusing on the senses increases the possibility of intimacy. Concentrating on the notion of yourself as a sensual person begins the process. Feeling your body as you move, and being aware of the interplay between clothes, air and skin during the course of the day, contributes to increasing sensuality. Non-sexual touch – such as stroking, tickling and hugging – eases the barrier between one person and another and can increase the possibility of trust and openness. Reading erotic or romantic books together can create a frisson. Watching movies that stimulate connection might also be a possibility, although, in general, TV in the bedroom is not recommended – it takes attention away from loving.

Emotionally

Undressing in front of another person in a sexual way is a very exposing thing to do; it can strip us of all our protective layers and reveal our authentic selves. In this way we leave ourselves open to judgement and rejection; this is perhaps why so many people drink alcohol before an intimate encounter.

But this vulnerability is the gateway to intimacy and pleasure, as letting go of control is essential for connection to happen. What stops this is often fear or self-criticism. A partner can close off the possibility of intimacy due to concern that their body is not desirable or because they do not want the other person to have access to their inner selves.

This is the difference between casual and intimate sex: in casual sex the partner does not know us, and so we are not giving the partner the power to reject the real us. In order to avoid closing ourselves off emotionally, we need to accept ourselves fully, allowing us to achieve a sense of wholeness, and part of that process is allowing someone else to accept us fully too. Sex in a long-term relationship allows us to truly expand and develop ourselves beyond our boundaries and, on occasion, to soar free.

Mentally

Sex can cause mental torture, in that the mind can fill up with ridiculous notions, instead of concentrating on the task at hand. Imagine your lover has his or her hand on your stomach, and the thought process goes something like this: 'I must start doing stomach exercises ... I wonder if I should eat less wheat to flatten it? ... What do I have that is wheat-free in the cupboard? ... I must go to the health food shop later today ...' These thoughts intensify with familiarity. Originally, we would not dream of losing focus with our beloved, but with years of being together our minds can drift in a millisecond.

There is an argument that sex happens in the brain, and

if your brain is elsewhere the sex is unlikely to be successful. In fact, a successful sexual encounter might entail letting go of thoughts almost completely. *Scientific American Mind* published a special collection on 'Your Sexual Brain' in 2009, in which Martin Portner reports that 'when a woman reached orgasm, something unexpected happened: much of her brain went silent'.[5] Thinking, planning, organising and minding all have to become muted for women to reach the peak of sexual pleasure. Thinking is a problem. Mindfulness is well known as a method of training the mind to be quiet; as this practice uses the physical body to connect to the present, it may well help us in training the mind to be quiet to allow intimacy to happen. Using the senses to focus the mind on the other person allows us to achieve full presence, and this is a precursor to intimacy. In other words, if your mind wanders, look, listen, touch, smell or taste your partner, and your mind will follow suit.

No-sex relationships

Sex in advertising and the media so bombards us that it can lead to the belief that everyone is having lots of sexual encounters. However, this is not necessarily the case, as it has been reported that people in the UK may be having less sex than they had a decade ago.[6] Many couples find that the amount of sex they are having has dwindled, or sex has

---

5   Portner, M., 'The Orgasmic Mind:', *Scientific American Mind*, Special Collection, 2009, p. 30.
6   Natsal-3, 'The National Survey of Sexual Attitudes and Lifestyles, UK, 2010–2013', www.natsal.ac.uk.

ceased altogether, and they struggle to find a way back to intimacy.

Sometimes there are underlying causes that were camouflaged by the power of the earlier hormonal surge, only to surface fully when the relationship is established and commitment is on the way. There are many reasons why a couple may stop having sex; some may be as simple as getting out of the habit, but many are more difficult to resolve. Among the possibilities are sexual abuse earlier in life, lack of desire due to trauma in earlier life, no ability to orgasm, seeing the partner as a father/mother as opposed to a lover, personal inhibitions or mental health issues. Human beings are complex, and there is nowhere more likely to exhibit our complexities than intimate relationships. If the couple are very comfortable and safe in their relationship, they may not tackle the lack of sex for many years; it may arise as an issue only when there is a desire to have a family or one person makes a complaint. A common reason that couples tolerate lack of sex is a desire to protect the loved one from hurt, embarrassment or blame; however, while this demonstrates love, it does not act in the best interests of the couple, as communication is restricted.

One of the exercises that may assist a couple to re-ignite a sex life involves using gradual sensualisation. One woman in her early sixties and newly involved in a no-sex relationship said, 'I am almost glad we had a problem, as it made us so much closer, talking about it and doing great connecting exercises.' (See *Exercise 8: Gradual sensualisation*.)

Another helpful exercise involves the sexual messages

lifeline – to help uncover past influences and difficulties. (See *Exercise 10: Sexual messages lifeline*.) However, if the exercise uncovers past trauma, it is a very good idea for the person or couple to look for help. The starting point can be a GP, counsellor or couples therapist.

Gender roles

As gender roles are becoming more enmeshed, there is a corresponding shift in sexual intimacy. Masculinity used to require that men take the active role and women the more passive, but this has changed considerably; women now demand a satisfying sexual life and men are, perhaps, feeling more pressured. Homosexual couples have a history and a language to help discuss gender roles in relationships, but heterosexual couples may be struggling to have the conversation. Men are now expected to be sympathetic and empathetic while being able to switch to the dominant, strong character in the bedroom – not only can this cause confusion, but the body might also react to this demand by shutting down completely.

Women, too, might be perturbed by the experience of being dominant in the boardroom but passive in the bedroom, and find that this no longer fits their version of themselves. The alternative to having a frank and real discussion about this is to shy away from intimacy and avoid the difficult conversations – the result can be emotional and physical distance. Martha (48) says:

> [When my husband] lost his job, I had to be very careful not
> to rock his sense of being the man. I would hide the bills so

he would not feel bad and be very sensitive to only looking for sex when he seemed to be in the mood – for fear of another experience of failure for him.

Most people have both active and passive aspects to their gender roles, and sexual intimacy allows a possibility for expressing both aspects.

The *Irish Times* survey asked all participants if they had felt attraction for someone of the same sex. They found that a quarter of heterosexual respondents said that they had experienced same-sex attraction; there were, however, stark differences between the sexes, with forty per cent of female participants saying they had felt same-sex attraction, compared with just fourteen per cent of men.[7] Perhaps women have more plasticity in their sexual response than men, but this finding might also point to a sexual continuum for everyone (straight to gay), with men preferring to stay at either end.

Common sexual problems for men

Erectile dysfunction is probably the most common problem for men, as the sales of drugs for the problem signify. The *Irish Times* survey reports that roughly a quarter of men in the age group seventeen to forty-nine had experienced erectile dysfunction, with the figure rising for those in the older age categories.[8]

In the past, it was mostly older men who suffered from erectile dysfunction, with a physical cause – such as diabetes

---

7   Holmquist, 'Let's Talk about Sex' (2015).
8   *Ibid.*

or heart difficulties – at its base. However, now younger men are presenting with dysfunction, and the cause can often be performance anxiety, driven by high expectations and fear of judgement. Early use of porn may also play its role in creating experiences that do not have human interaction at their core. Often the problem is exacerbated by avoidance of sexual intimacy for years and then finding that telling the truth is too wide a gap to bridge. Following a bad experience, it may take years for someone to risk being sexually intimate with another human being; in many cases, the longer the gap, the more difficult the re-engagement. Fionn (25) says:

> My first experience of sex was excruciating. I couldn't come, and the longer it went on the worse I felt. It didn't help that [my former partner] later put up on Facebook that I was a dud. I haven't had the guts to risk sex with someone since.

Luckily, the power of desire is that it drives a person to connect with another, so it acts as a strong push to risk connection and disclosure with a potential partner. Most people find that their partner is understanding and supportive – plus being relieved that it is not their own lack of attractiveness that is at the root of the problem. When two people tackle the problem, there is twice the effectiveness, with the added bonus of honesty, trust and empathy embedding itself at the core of the relationship. Again, the starting point in overcoming the issue is a visit to the GP to check if there is a physical problem and then, perhaps, getting some professional support. In addition, it is worth consulting Bernie

Zilbergeld's *The New Male Sexuality* – a very useful book containing many exercises and suggestions.[9]

Lack of desire has surfaced as another difficulty for men; so, too, have retarded or premature ejaculation. A joint approach of medical and psychological investigation is often the best option in addressing these difficulties, as many men need to check that there is no physical basis for the issue before they look for more alternative clues. The chances are that there is a complex root to the difficulty, and the longer the problem lies unexamined the more avoidance there is in tackling it.

Men often have a 'fix it' approach; their idea is that they need to be 'fixed' before engaging in a relationship. However, this is often not the best approach, as the way forward often includes investigation, discussion and risking the vulnerability that a relationship can offer. Medication, recreational drugs, lifestyle and eating habits can all contribute to sexual functioning, and desire is often a reflection of the kind of life the person is living. Mental health is also reflected in sexual well-being, and all efforts to promote this will have an effect; for example, if people are suffering from depression they are unlikely to be interested in or able to respond to sexual desire. The main message for men is, first, to acknowledge that there is a problem, and, second, to seek medical assessment, as there might be an underlying issue that needs attention. Following this, a referral to a professional working in the area of sexual difficulty might be a good idea. Inviting the

---

9   Zilbergeld, B., *The New Male Sexuality* (revised edition, Bantam Books, New York, 1999).

partner, if there is one, to go along as well can be beneficial. Because men tend not to speak to one another about this type of issue, they have no idea just how common sexual difficulties are. They often suffer alone, without the support or expertise that are easily available.

Women's sexual difficulties

Women experience many sexual difficulties, and there is no age when difficulty might not present itself. Common experiences are pain during intercourse, vaginismus (the vagina closes), lack of orgasm, lack of desire or arousal, lack of masturbatory capacity or combinations of these.

Forty-three per cent of women across all age categories reported having experienced an inability to orgasm in the *Irish Times* survey.[10] This demonstrated the commonality of sexual difficulties, and revealed the inaccuracy of the idea that only older age groups suffer in this way. Again, many women work from the assumption that things will improve when the right partner comes along; often, however, the pattern deepens, and instead of things improving, the fear of failure adds to the difficulty. This can, in turn, lead to avoidance and self-criticism. Going to a GP or women's health clinic is the beginning of the road to recovery; there is usually an added psychological component, however, and it is likely that the self-commentary about the difficulty can be harsh, pessimistic and continuous. There is no doubt that the comments we have in our heads are uncontested and are

---

10 Holmquist, 'Let's Talk about Sex' (2015).

not usually up for discussion with others, but these comments can have devastating effects on our lives. Consider the effect on a woman holding strongly held beliefs such as, 'I am damaged goods. No one will ever love me, and there is no point in trying to solve it because I know nothing will work.' Every time this woman gets into a sexual encounter, she will withdraw into herself so as not to upset her partner; the result will be to block desire from working and the couple will lose out on the chance of intimacy. New drugs are coming onto the market that may help women to tackle some of their sexual difficulties. There is strong evidence that intervention can be very successful: gynaecological expertise together with physiotherapy and psychotherapy are all recommended, and the earlier the intervention, the better the possible outcome.

Many women believe that male partners will not be capable of dealing with a sexual difficulty, but this is erroneous; many men have proven their patience, protectiveness and faith in the relationship by being consistent and loyal through the recovery pathway. Having a good women's health book is a very good start; there are many excellent selections available. Because depression or anxiety often accompany sexual difficulty, it is important to take someone (a friend or sister, perhaps) into your confidence; this will give you a sounding board to check the level of help you need and the support to see you through the process.

Disparate sexual drives
Many couples experience matching sex drives in the early phases of their relationship and assume this will continue.

However, numerous couples report a disparity in their sex drive; the *Irish Times* survey found that only one-third of respondents believe that they are on an even keel with their partner sexually. Two-thirds of male respondents said that their sex drive was higher than their partner's, but a quarter of women rated their sex drive as being the higher.[11] It seems that the longer the relationship lasts, the wider the gap in sex drive. This is a big issue for couples, and often rows or resentment result. The key seems to be being brave and having the conversation. It is necessary to take into account each partner's needs, and perhaps this is the direction to take. One partner might want sex every day, but the other person's wish for no pressure might take precedence; another time the partner's request for sex and connection might be the bigger need, and so the couple prioritises that. This will require a lot of discussion, understanding and empathy, which can only serve to make the relationship stronger.

We have become more adventurous in our sexual activity. Fifty-eight per cent of couples in the *Irish Times* survey report using sex toys at some point. Oral sex is now part of normal sexual activity, and anal sex and BDSM (bondage, discipline, submission and masochism) all play their part in the sexual landscape. While these activities are not mainstream, one in five participants reported engaging in them. This is not a small number and shows that there is an interest in having an interesting sex life and a trust in the partner who participates with us.[12]

---

11 *Ibid.*
12 *Ibid.*

Sex can lead to a more intimate life with your partner, but it is not the only pathway to this. Affection, trust, honesty and loyalty have huge roles to play in laying down the foundations of a relationship. Being able to talk about sex is the first step to intimacy, regardless of the outcome. It takes courage to have the conversation, but the possible benefit is lots more fun, pleasure, playfulness and imagination – in other words, living better.

7

Porn and relationships

The entire Internet is in a sense pornographic, a deliverer of constant excitement that we have no innate capacity to resist, a seducer that leads us down paths that for the most part do nothing to answer our real needs. Furthermore the ready availability of pornography lessens our tolerance for the kind of boredom that grants our mind the space it needs to spawn good ideas ...

Alain de Botton[1]

In *A Billion Wicked Thoughts*, Ogi Ogas and Sai Gaddam apply a scientific research lens to the topic of porn, and the result is enlightening, funny and quirky. As the title implies, there have been billions of views of porn online, and this allows heretofore unseen access to people's sexual desires and fantasies. Ogas and Gaddam enquire as to how diverse human sexual interests might be:

> Not very diverse, it turns out. Just twenty different interests account for 80% of all searches. That's rather remarkable. With less than two dozen interests, you can satisfy the desires of almost everyone who uses a search engine to find erotic content.[2]

---

1   De Botton (2012), p. 102.
2   Gaddam, S. and Ogas, O., *A Billion Wicked Thoughts: What the World's*

The most popular sexual search category by far is 'Youth', with the second search being 'Gay' and the third 'MILFs'.[3] No matter how unusual people might find their sexual preference, if you type it into a search engine, there will be others with the same preference. Alain de Botton comments:

> Pornographic-content providers [have] exploited a design flaw of the male gender. A mind originally designed to cope with little more sexually tempting than the occasional sight of a tribeswoman across the savannah is rendered helpless when bombarded by continual invitations to participate in erotic scenarios far exceeding any dreamt of by the diseased mind of the Marquis de Sade.[4]

Ogas and Gaddam claim that men's sexual cues are imprinted during puberty and remain steady throughout life, while women's sexual cues are more varied. This means that men need one sexual cue for desire and response to happen, whereas woman may have many cues to be met before sexual desire can be satisfied. Ogas and Gaddam add: 'For many men one particular cue can be absolutely essential for arousal, which is the reason why fetishes are so much more common in men than in women. But for most women, no single cue is essential to activate arousal.'[5] Women may need many psychological, emotional and physical cues to be met.

Largest Experiment Reveals about Human Desire (Plume, New York, 2012), p. 17.

3   *Ibid.*, p. 16.

4   De Botton (2012), p. 97.

5   Gaddam and Ogas (2012), p. 124.

There has been a continuous divergence in how men's and women's brains have developed in response to their sexual needs. Men tend to focus on the genitals in porn, while women are interested in facial expression and the story. Erotica for men is visual, while for women it is multifaceted and often includes romance. Many women will say that reading romantic books improves their sex lives with their partners, but they would doubt that their men watching porn might have the same effect. According to Gaddam and Ogas, 'Though many women feel betrayed when their partners watch porn, they rarely feel that they are betraying their husbands by reading romance.'[6] Table 1 shows the preferred online sexual activity of men and women.[7]

Table 1: Preferred online sexual activity of men and women

Preferred online sexual activity	% of men	% of women
Viewing erotic pictures and movies	37	6
Staying in contact with love/sex partners	8	21
Reading erotic stories	6	9

Human sexuality is very diverse, with homosexuality, bisexuality and transsexuality appearing often alongside heterosexuality in the course of human history. It is hard for us to accept that other people's most intimate desires might be different from our own; at many times over the period of

6   *Ibid.*, p. 171.
7   *Ibid.*, p. 19.

recent history some sexual activities have been banned or outlawed (for example masturbation, oral or anal sex and homosexuality). The Internet has demonstrated the breadth of human desire, but there has always been a fear that this might get out of control. As Gaddam and Ogas point out, 'Historically, male exhibitionism has been considered a mental disorder. If that is the case, the Internet suggests we are a planet of mentally deranged men.'[8]

Whereas there is a fear around the proliferation of porn, there is the caveat that humans' conscious thinking minds can figure out the pattern of their own cues and their responses to it. In the words of Gaddam and Ogas: 'We can accept our fantasies without becoming slaves to them.'[9] The argument against this might be our almost complete lack of ability to talk to others in any meaningfully way about our use or experience of porn.

In a recent survey, more than four out of every five participants said they had used pornography in their lifetime; the division between men and women was ninety-six per cent to sixty-nine per cent.[10] Of that number, eleven per cent of men said they watched it every day (compared with one per cent of women), with more than fifty per cent of men saying they watched it once a week. The allure of the Internet is powerful; the fact that porn is available on all our devices is almost too much to resist. Alain de Botton suggests:

---

8   *Ibid.*, p. 42.
9   *Ibid.*, p. 241.
10 Holmquist, K., 'When Porn becomes a Problem', Weekend Review, *The Irish Times*, 8 August 2015.

Whenever we feel an all but irresistible desire to flee from our own thoughts, we can be quite sure there is something important trying to make its way into our consciousness – and yet it is precisely at such pregnant moments that Internet pornography is most apt to exert its maddening pull, assisting our escape from ourselves and thereby helping us to destroy our present and our future.[11]

Young men and porn

Men, in particular, are hooked into porn at a young age, as their sexual curiosity and their desire to have knowledge of sex before the fact drives them to the Internet. Many of the games they play on the Internet have little icons popping up inviting them to view porn. Also, simple things such as typing 'boobs' into a search engine can, in seconds, have full sex on screen. Often, these young males are in fact boys who have yet to experience puberty; it is unlikely they will go to their parents to discuss what they have seen. This can have a complex effect on their burgeoning sexuality, with desire and suppression (fear of getting caught) happening simultaneously. Most young men say that they are handling their own use of porn, but they would like to prevent this exposure from happening to other very young boys.

Katie Doherty, in a study entitled 'Effects of Accessing Sexually Explicit Online Materials on Young Irish Males' Sexual Attitudes, Knowledge and Behaviours', found that there appeared to be a desire to open up and discuss the

---

11 De Botton (2012), p. 102.

topic of porn seriously.[12] The young men responded well to black-and-white (or direct) questions (they said that parents tended to talk about porn in the abstract or third person, and this was not effective). They commented that they would like to have information on types of porn, as the different types being watched led to problems: rape porn, child or teen porn, or specific porn (such as date-rape porn) caused concern. The shame and isolation caused by these types of porn often led to social and emotional problems.

All the young men asserted that porn was fake, false and unrealistic. They suggested that the porn lacked intimacy and some disclosed that they would like more relationship education as part of the broader sex-education in schools. There were comments that real live sex is becoming more porn-like and performance pressure was a result. Lee (20) said, 'I feel I have to be the dominant one – a task to do rather than an expression of something.'

It also appears that the more people watched porn, the more mistakes they made – that is the more misinformation they believed. Believing misinformation can create blurred lines, such as 'When does "No" mean "Yes"?' In most porn, 'No' is always a precursor to 'Yes', and this can lead to unintended consequences.

A couple reported issues regarding trust and their relationship following an incident in which the guy did not stop

---

12 Doherty, K., 'Effects of Accessing Sexually Explicit Online Materials on Young Irish Males' Sexual Attitudes, Knowledge and Behaviours' (Masters in Psychological Science thesis, University of Limerick, unpublished, 2013).

anal sex when asked to – he said that he knew his porn watching had created this possibility, and he had never thought of himself previously as an insensitive or aggressive person.

Sex always needs to be consensual; it is necessary to highlight this more in relationships.

Porn and addiction

For a percentage of men and a smaller percentage of women, porn can become very addictive and have all the usual addictive consequences. It can take over thoughts, hours and lives and, as it is such a solitary activity, it can lead to social isolation and an inability to relate to the potential partners in any meaningful manner. The availability of ever-increasing hits can lead to the seeking of more degrading forms of sexual activity; this can result in shame and further withdrawal from partners or families. Deceit is usually part and parcel of this process, and relationships can be torn asunder as a result.

Rachel, quoted in *The Irish Times*, says of her sex-addicted partner:

> They will do it right under your nose on their laptops and phones. It's the lying – even when they are discovered, there is no contrition, they are devoid of empathy at that point. And it escalates as they move on to more and more extreme material, then turn to the purchase of women for sex.[13]

---

13 Holmquist, 'When Porn Becomes a Problem' (2015).

There is a very familiar situation with many couples: the woman goes to bed and the man then goes online for a number of hours. It may well be that the woman is not interested in sex and the man can argue that he is not causing her any irritation; the effect on the couple, however, can be estrangement and loneliness. Both people are suffering. Discussion and the willingness to be vulnerable in front of your partner are the beginnings of finding a way through this difficulty. We often assume that there is a 'bad and good' aspect to this situation, but in fact it might be that much more basic human needs are involved. Maltz and Maltz, in the book *The Porn Trap*, comment:

> Because using porn often involves high levels of dishonesty and secrecy, those who are caught up in it often say they feel isolated, ashamed, depressed, phony, morally compromised, and even in some cases, suicidal. Many are angry, irritable and unable to sleep. Some tell us porn is leading them on a dangerous path into illegal and risky activities, such as viewing child pornography, having affairs, having anonymous sex at adult bookstores, hiring prostitutes and viewing porn at work.[14]

When someone's whole life is being affected by porn use, it is time to get help from the professionals, as this can be a very difficult issue to tackle alone. The support of a family or partner can be crucial, but it is likely that the partner may also require help. The partner, too, may have suffered in the process.

---

14 Maltz, W. and Maltz, L., *The Porn Trap* (HarperCollins, New York, 2010), p. 2.

Female partners of heavy users of porn

As in any addiction, in porn addiction the activity becomes more important than anything else in the person's life, and so it may have all the associated effects on the partner: betrayal, complete loss of trust, anger and abandonment. Women often feel threatened by the sexual acts depicted in porn and the degrading roles to which women are subjected. Women worry that their partner might expect them to do these things and they might have deep reservations about it; however, they are also worried that if they refuse they may be seen as prudish or lose the relationship completely. Women and men react to the perceived messages in porn via their own cues, and this can lead to division and misunderstanding. Naturally, women react to the violence inherent in porn, but men don't necessarily react in the same way. Women can feel betrayed by porn – by the fact that their men prefer looking at porn to intimacy with them, or that their bodies are being unfavourably compared to those online. This feeling of betrayal can have a negative effect on a woman's sense of attractiveness and on her sense of security in a relationship.

Male partners often deny or play down their use of porn, and so women can become investigators, and develop suspicion and checking as part of the relationship. The result is often breakdown, as the game of hiding, protesting innocence and fear of being made a fool of become central to the relationship. As men try to change their porn habit, their partners might take each setback personally; the men may not want to cause further upset or hurt, so they hide their failures, and the situation continues as before. Women who have had this experience often bring the sense of suspicion into the next relationship, fearing that they can trust no man. Then the next relationship is already vulnerable before it starts. Maggie (31) says:

> I know it's mad, but I check the web history and his phone compulsively, and I even find myself making excuses to drop in unannounced if I am out for the evening – just to see if he is online. I know I am driving him crazy.

In this situation, both partners need help in changing their responses to and habits regarding intimacy, fantasy and porn.

Female and gay users of porn

Gay men watch more porn than straight men, and they are also more comfortable talking about porn. Gay men are also more tolerant than are women of their partners watching porn: 'The gay brain seems to be loaded with the same visual desire software as the straight brain – except that the gay visual cues target male bodies instead of female bodies.'[15] Women too watch porn, as the *Irish Times* survey recorded, but they watch it less often than men. Women are also more likely to watch porn with a partner, with twenty per cent of female participants saying they watched it with someone else, compared to just four per cent of male users. There is a growing number of women looking to satisfy their erotic

---

15 Gaddam and Ogas (2012), p. 139.

tastes online, as this is now a complex private activity and there is no need to go to an adult shop. There is an argument that women are tired of the very male focus of online porn, but that has been corrected by the arrival of female-orientated porn sites such as makelovenotporn.tv. However, there is a consistent number of female porn users who like the same porn that men like, and – as is the case with men – these women are subject to the same addiction and obsessive possibilities.

Tanya Sweeney, writing about women and porn, says her friend came up with the perfect analogy: 'Porn is a bit like cake.' She says:

> I've been raised to know that a little bit of cake is perfectly okay as part of a healthy and balanced diet of breakfast, lunch and dinner. But then, we didn't grow up with all the cake in the world behind an unlocked door, right next door to our bedroom. Imagine how that would be?[16]

What to do about the use of porn

Psychotherapist Dermod Moore is quoted as saying:

> We avoid talk in Irish culture that is sex-positive; by which I mean honestly and directly. Yes there is plenty of it about; it's in the media, but the hardest thing of all, it seems, is to bring up the topic of sex in a way that is not comic, or shame-filled, or needing Dutch courage to address it.

16 Sweeney, T., 'It's Complicated: The Truth about Women and Porn', *The Irish Times*, 20 January 2015.

Practically all men have used porn; how many have discussed it openly?[17]

Open discussion is clearly a great starting point, but talking about sex – and porn use in particular – requires courage and stepping over many vulnerabilities and fears. We should bring up conversations in as many ways as possible: sitting at the bar with a friend, over the family dinner, in bed with our loved one or talking to a parent. No one has the perfect stance, but through discussion we might come to understand everybody's position and have a chance to hear ourselves talk with both trepidation and honesty. Then, perhaps, young people might trust the older group to handle such a discussion and not just adopt either a liberal or a conservative position. Husbands who have hidden their porn or sexual activity for years might be able to consider coming out in the open about it and be their authentic selves, without risking total rejection. Women might be able to let go of the veneer of 'I'm fine with porn', and have their fears and concerns really heard and not derided.

Eroticism is an essential part of life, as even ancient cave drawings have shown: it allows us to strip bare our defences and let go of control in a way that life does not easily offer us. As Edward Abbey has been quoted as saying, 'Modern men and women are obsessed with the sexual; it is the only realm of primordial adventure still left to most of us.'[18] Allowing ourselves to create and enjoy erotica is one of the great

---

17 Quoted in Holmquist, 'When Porn becomes a Problem' (2015), p. 1.
18 Quoted in Gaddam and Ogas (2012), p. 241.

pleasures for human beings; we need to be conscious of the many ways we can generate this. That porn is available at the touch of a button might operate against our imaginations and thus our sensual encounters are the lesser for it.

Revenge porn

At the beginning of many relationships, couples regularly send pictures on smartphones of themselves in erotic poses. This is playful, teasing and suggestive, and it assumes confidentiality and trust in the relationship. However, there is now quite a trend for jilted lovers to post naked or suggestive pictures of their ex on websites dedicated to so-called 'revenge porn' and to accompany the images with nasty commentary. This elicits much other comment and can be highly derogatory and libellous. As this occurs in open view, the victim's work colleagues, children, family and friends are often able to access the material, and it can cause enormous distress and embarrassment. The victim, and not the perpetrator, often feels the blame and shame in these cases.

It is true to say that the victim of revenge porn has nothing to be ashamed of; but saying this does not take the sting out of other people having access to your intimate life. The message has to be not to send revealing pictures of yourself until you are sure of the relationship and you know you can completely trust your partner. As Padraig O'Morain states:

> … even when the image is made with the consent of whoever is depicted, how is it right or fair that these moments of lust-driven gullibility should be punished by sustained public

humiliation? And how fair is it that the smirking rat behind it all should be able to inflict this humiliation on his ex without consequences for himself?

Not right or fair at all. Bring on the law.[19]

It is easy to blame the medium for the problems we encounter, but of course it is our use of the medium that is within our control. There was a time when the fears of the effects of TV on the population were the subject of serious public debate, and we now look back on that with amusement. As human beings, we are naturally curious and interested in expanding in every way possible, and there is often a pendulum swing with the newest fad. Most people will find a level of comfort over time with their use of technology, but there is no doubt that many people are currently suffering, and they are continuing without any understanding or support. The eroticism or porn discussion needs to move from a good-or-bad debate to a more nuanced, curious and open exchange. This should happen at both the private and public levels.

---

19 O'Morain, P., 'That's Men: "Revenge Porn" could be classified in law as a form of cyberbullying', Health Section, *The Irish Times*, 25 November 2014, p. 11.

8

Endings or breaches: moving forward

> Getting married is easy. Staying married is more difficult. Staying happily married for a lifetime must be considered among the fine arts.
>
> *Roberta Flack*[1]

'Saucer-effect' relationships

Many couples spend years in relationships in which they experience what I call the 'saucer effect'. They are neither in the relationship nor out of it. Think of their relationship as a saucer – they circle each other in a kind of limbo on the edges of it. They get stuck in a place where they cannot trust or care or lust after each other enough to go right to the centre, or they do not dislike each other enough to break out over the edge of the saucer and leave. They can develop an endurance for this over the years, and can find this habit more and more difficult to challenge; at all times, however, one or both will feel dissatisfied, unhappy and unfulfilled. Very often a crisis will break the stalemate – for example an affair, illness, trauma with a child – but it is not unusual for the couple to

---

1   As quoted in Henriques, S. M., *God Can Handle It … Marriage* (Walnut Grove, Nashville, 2010), p. 138.

address the crisis and return to the familiarity of the edge of the saucer and continue the situation. They may use all kinds of issues to demonstrate the lack of commitment, and sex, money and families of origin can become areas of tetchiness and anger. Usually one person tries to rescue the situation, but this effort ends in frustration as it is not sustained for long enough, or the other partner is oblivious to the person's efforts.

This couple often have a lot in common and started out with similar goals. Their shared ideals are strong; perhaps this is what makes it very difficult for them to give up on the situation. These values might be ambition in terms of work, raising a family or having a joint community that holds them together. Sometimes one person seeks his or her own self-development and gains self-awareness and knowledge of the situation, but finds it too difficult to let go of the relationship. This person still has the connection that was so strong in the early relationship; he or she may see that the other partner is stressed or stuck and not want to leave the partner in this state, or may want to protect their children from the pain of separation, or may fear making a mistake and regretting it in the future, or may simply not have the economic freedom to risk breaking-up.

Whatever the reason, the ongoing pattern is set. It will continue unless there is a crisis. Sometimes this crisis can reverberate outwards and cause harm to lots of people. Children can end up mediating between parents and living in houses where martyrdom and silence are normalised. Sometimes, the partners seek their emotional connections elsewhere, and all the intimacy is happening outside the relationship. A partner can feel very isolated and shut down to the extent of being unable to express his or her fear of loss, and therefore go unheard. And all this can be exacerbated and maintained by habit, lack of awareness and an inability to broach the reality because of fear. Maria (45) explains:

> There was nothing too bad to complain about. We had a nice house and enough money and the kids were in good schools, but there was something huge missing and my partner would not talk about it. Over the years we became like business partners, and even though we shared the same bed there was no chance of sex or romance. It knocked the spark out of me, and I stopped seeing myself as desirable or even as someone worth talking to. In retrospect, I think my husband was suffering from mild depression for years, but he wouldn't talk about it or get help, and it broke me in the end.

The seven-year review

Of course, the earlier a saucer-effect situation is acknowledged and tackled, the better. It is unlikely that a couple in this situation will resolve it without some outside intervention, and any external person asking questions will outline the reality very quickly. If the couple is to break this stalemate situation, it will require all the habit-breaking skills outlined earlier, as well as the tackling of avoidance and the facing of possible conflict.

There is some merit to the argument that all relationships should come up for review every seven years. Seven years is a period of time that is mythologised – in the phrase 'seven-year itch', for example – and so it might represent a block of time in a relationship. The couple could put aside a time and place to meet and make a case for why and how they should stay together for the next seven years – both could reflect and review and then meet again to give their responses. They might even ask those close to the relationship for comments.

The core of this is honesty and fearlessness, and, of course, there is the inherent danger that one partner might refuse to commit for the next seven years. There are some aspects that might be helpful, however. If we are being reviewed for promotion or demotion in our jobs, we are more conscious of what we are doing and of the standard we are reaching and of what we are aiming for in the future. It wakes us up and makes us choose how we spend our lives. This aliveness is missing from the saucer relationships. There is no doubt that having a push off the edge of the saucer will create something new.

Break-up

Laura (31) describes falling in love with someone at work. She says that for a long time there was no attraction and then it just happened. She explains that she loved spending time with her workmate and thought this could be someone she could have a future with. He ended it by saying, 'We really need to talk about us. Do you think it is working out?' and added that they would talk about it in the future, but he never did. Laura describes that time as 'heart-breaking

– I hated the limbo of not knowing where I stood, it wasn't right.' This was compounded by the difficulty and rejection of seeing him at work every day and exacerbated when he started going out with someone else in the office: 'They kept laughing together and it cracked me up.' Laura says that moving to a new job was the beginning of recovery and that it takes a year to get over such heartache, but that friends want you to be over it much faster. There are lingering effects: 'I now go into a dating situation and I think it won't last, and I'm waiting for the exit.'

There is no doubt that a break-up is traumatic, even if you are the person instigating it. It can often take years to come fully through such rejection, but people do. If they are aware enough, they do not repeat the same pattern.

Nigel (50) separated from his wife – against his will – when she left three years ago. He says:

> I am almost grateful to her now as I have never been happier, and if she had stayed I would not know how great I could feel. I am dating someone now who is mad about me, and I feel as if a darkness has been lifted off me that I did not even realise was there.

Adam (25) is still raw from the aftermath of his girlfriend's sudden departure – she left a note on his bed in their apartment and disappeared. He can see that the signs were there, but he says that he is an 'incurable romantic' and he thought that if he put in enough effort he could make it work. Adam is not sure if he will experience this again, as he wants to believe in the power of love, but he is committed to being cautious for a long time.

Very often the signs of a break-up are present long before the actual event, but we push them out of the way in favour of the idea that 'love will conquer all'. The feeling of rejection can be so powerful that it can take a long time to apply analysis to the situation and see it clearly. This period of time is full of grief and longing, and having the person in your vicinity or in your social group can make it worse. The jilted partners can pour pain into their own wounds by looking up their ex's Facebook page and seeing what a good life the ex is having or who the ex is dating now. In other cases, the rejected person can create a pretend virtual life by posting personal pictures of them having fun with beautiful partners – with the sole aim of getting the ex to feel he or she has made a huge mistake.

Grief

The truth is that grief has to be borne. It has to be gone through and suffered and the more willing you are to engage in that process, the earlier release from it will come. We need good people around us, who can tolerate our abject loss and still be there. We need the ordinary comforting things of life: cups of tea, movies, duvet days and ice cream. We need to go home to our families and have our dinners made and have long walks in sympathising rain. It will pass, but it will take whatever time it requires; our hastening of that time does not always have a good effect.

The desire to get away from grief can have a postponing

effect. Drowning our sorrows, taking drugs, losing ourselves in one-night stands all offer only temporary relief, and the real work is still waiting to be started. Talking, sharing stories, ranting and crying can all be therapeutic. It is better that we do these things in company so that we don't resort to texting the ex-partner or sink into depression. No one escapes grief in life, and while it can make you feel very isolated, there is always someone who can understand and empathise. Physical activity can help – not just as a way of stopping your mind from going over the whole relationship again, but also by making you feel and look better, and boosting your confidence. When we are full of grief, it is hard to face the world, and we often retreat into our homes and heads. Committing to some physical activity will force us to participate, shift the apathy and get us to engage with the human race again. While it is not the answer, it is part of the pathway.

Affairs

Affairs are sometimes secret, sometimes exposed, sometimes told and always traumatic. They are not always what you think they are, and they do not always spell the end of a relationship. They can be a wake-up call, or denote an existential crisis, a response to a personal drama, a fear of commitment, a lust unabated or an expression of boredom. The one part of an affair that is constant is the secrecy, and people often describe this deceit as the worst part of it. There are cultural differences in levels of acceptance of affairs, and indeed there are differences in family acceptance of affairs.

Imagine growing up in a family where a parent has been having an affair for years and it is tolerated for the greater good of the family – a child of this family will have a very different experience of affairs than a person whose family circumstances were different. Secrets, too, have differing cultural and personal acceptance. Some cultures define love as total transparency, while others allow more leeway, so the levels of betrayal felt can vary according to custom. All this points to the fact that affairs are very personal to the couple, and there are many understandings of them and many approaches to them.

Nowadays, technology plays a huge role in exposing affairs. Location apps on smartphones, mobile phone bills, email history and unexplained credit card bills have all been used in tracking the life of affairs. The reason someone goes looking for evidence is that they pick up a feeling of their partner gone missing or perhaps overcompensating. Strangely, an affair can also have the effect of making a partner more loving and sex better than when the affair was not happening.

The exposure of the affair, whether voluntary or involuntary, creates a moment or pause in the relationship; there is stocktaking and investigation of how this came about and why. Sometimes, when a person voluntarily admits the affair, there is a belief that the couple should get it over with quickly, and the term 'move on' is used regularly. However, the admission of the affair also represents an opportunity for growth in the relationship and in each individual person; and if they don't take this opportunity, there can be a return to something like the saucer effect mentioned above.

We can have a courtroom approach to dealing with affairs, with a desire for the crime to be read out, the person having the affair suitably admonished and, if possible, punishment applied, or at least a period of restitution set. If this is not available to us, the pathway to forgiveness, understanding and normality can be much more complex. Very often, whole communities are involved, with children, siblings, neighbours and friendship groups all deeply affected and invested in the outcome of the affair. It can be difficult to track the journey to the point of infidelity, to lay out both people's participation in that, and look at what needs repairing and how that might happen. All this assumes that the couple choose to stay together and try to mend the relationship rather than abandon it. In my experience, many people are not willing to give up on their commitment, certainly at the first transgression. What can happen, however, is that there is not enough insight or discussion in this first situation, and things go underground, only to surface again in another affair or some other trauma sometime later.

People do not always have affairs because there is something terribly wrong in their relationship; they might be having a crisis of existence, wondering if 'this is it', or they might find that the affair represents a rebellion against life. The affair can be facilitated by boredom and opportunity, with the perpetrator genuinely saying, 'It didn't mean anything.' However, the affair results in betrayal, hurt of a chosen life partner and, possibly, the loss of a whole way of life. An affair can represent the final phase of a long ending to a relationship, when the person who has the affair only discovers that the relationship is really over when he or she is in the arms of someone else. Whatever the situation, an admission of an affair requires a response, action and the engagement of both parties. If that doesn't happen – for example, when a woman has an affair in front of her partner's nose and the partner does not respond – then it is likely that there is very little to salvage and separation is inevitable. In no-sex marriages, the affair might present a challenge and an invitation to return to intimacy. There are possibly as many meanings to affairs as there are to relationships.

One good piece of advice is not to make a decision regarding the response to an affair too quickly. When we are in emotional pain and full of anger and resentment, we are unlikely to be able to make decisions that utilise our wisdom and judgement. Giving yourself time and space to recover, considering all the options, and seeking advice from those very close to you all offer you the best chance of making a decision that will be long-lasting and to your benefit. If you cannot talk to your partner in any kind of reasonable fashion due to heightened emotions, it is a good idea to take some time apart and agree to meet to discuss things in a short space of time. The important thing here is to organise that meeting and to turn up for it and any subsequent meetings. It is best if these conversations happen in a neutral venue so that passions do not rise; even if you are the person who has chosen to leave, the other partner deserves to have his or her questions answered and to be allowed some attempt at closure. How we end relationships is often a measure of the kind of character we are; most of us would like to be seen as honest, courageous and considerate.

Divorce

In Ireland, nearly one in ten marriages ends in separation or divorce. This is low by European standards, and it has not dented the popularity of marriage – the number of both church and civil services continues to rise, according to a report by Kate Holmquist.[2] John Farrelly, quoted in the same report, says:

> ... marital commitment and the willingness to put up with unhappiness in order to stay married are in the Irish DNA ... People stay married for many years longer than they should. They've driven each other mad and are at the point of losing their minds by the time they consider divorce.[3]

The adversarial nature of divorce can create years of intense engagement in a very negative sense, with each of the couple gathering evidence and support for his or her position that the other is evil. This can drain a couple of all their finances and destroy their friendship group, but the real damage here is to the children. Most people are aware that children's needs should be central to the discussion, but placing them at the centre can be very difficult when another accusatory letter arrives on the doorstep. The reality is that the couple will need to have an ongoing relationship as parents of their children, and they will both need to attend school functions, conferences, weddings, baptisms and the like for the duration

---

2   Holmquist, K., 'Divorce, Irish Style', Weekend Review, *The Irish Times*, 17 January 2015.

3   *Ibid.*, p. 1.

of their lives. It is worth considering this during the process of the divorce, as the early confrontations can lead to lifelong aggressive or subversive engagements.

Mediation is recognised as an 'agreed' solution to the difficulties of divorce. Current statistics suggest that forty-three per cent of couples who attend mediation reach agreement.[4] If the couple can take some of the animosity out of the situation, then the children can act as children and not as mediators of conflict, and both parties have more emotional freedom to move on. There are stories of couples remaining friends; while these stories are rare, they can act as a template for others.

Anne (17) says, 'I have four parents now as both my parents remarried, and while I still like living with my Mum more, I love staying with my Dad too. I get two summer holidays while lots of my friends get one!'

Divorce has many stories of bitterness and unfairness. However, for those who have gone through it there may eventually be some redemption, as these words of one divorced woman indicate: 'Divorce is not easy. But it is easier than being married and stuck in a rut where I imagined no future, no real change and no way out. Divorce is also about growth and the complete acceptance of change.'[5]

For many people a period of time – between two and seven years – is the measure of recovery from a separation

---

4   *Ibid.* The Family Mediation Service is state run and can be found under the aegis of the Legal Aid Board.
5   'Claire: Divorce is about Growth and Change', in 'Divorced Ireland: The Readers Write', News Review, *The Irish Times*, 24 January 2015, p. 3.

or divorce. Of course, some of this mourning period can be happening while still in the relationship, but it usually takes longer than we think to feel fully alive and confident again. It may also take this amount of time to recover from the financial hit that divorce entails, but most people can begin considering a new relationship within this timeframe.

Blended families

We are now for the first time realising that there is such a thing as 'blended families', with two people at the centre of the family, but also perhaps children from both their previous relationships, plus ex-partners and their children, and perhaps children from the new relationship. The ensuing relationships can be complex and daunting – even when the children are adults and have left home. There is lots of room for rivalry, division and upset, and life in a blended family can feel like walking on eggshells when everyone gets together.

There is no template for this situation, as we are only now getting to grips with the implications of these new families. Who is invited to family events? Where do people sit? Who has the prominent role? These are all questions that can cause anxiety and panic. For college-going offspring, the following may be issues: In whose house do I have a room to call my own? Who helps me with finances? Who cares about me the most? Do I still have a home to go to and be a child in? Families and couples are negotiating these issues, but there are also many supports available: child-guidance clinics, family therapy and counselling services are all becoming more expert in these situations. There is a new richness to the tapestry of family, as all types of family are included and protected by our society. We may need to stretch old rituals and customs to accommodate the new reality of families, and this is what an evolving society is all about.

Living alone

Not everyone takes the path of moving into a new couple or family situation following separation or divorce, and many people live alone for long periods of their lives. The challenge is to make this a vibrant and full life and not allow it to become dull and withdrawn. Working or being engaged in something meaningful outside the home is vital to well-being. Accepting the losses and focusing on the good relationships that are already in existence will enrich life: being a wonderful aunt or uncle, having an interest in the local community, volunteering with other motivated people, for example, can all create a life worth living. If you have ever loved, the chances are that you know how to do this, and keeping that door open for the future is essential.

Jeff (70), whose wife died fifteen years ago, is dating again and finding that there is a buzz and thrill in this new adventure. The first step to a connection may well be the disclosure of loneliness; as this is such a recognised human trait, most people can connect with it. The second step may be using the Internet for online dating, no matter what age you are. As long as we are alive, relationships are central to our well-being and happiness. Ray (thirty-six years married) says, 'Realising that life is about relationships is key.'

Developing resilience

Developing resilience in the face of chosen, or forced, change is well worth aiming for, but most of us do not gain this wisdom until we are in the middle of the situation. Our responses to negative situations are often those of resentment, anger and vengeance; while these might be natural responses initially, if they continue, we create a self that is out of our control. This means that the other person – the one who hurt us – has control over our emotions, and we feel that we cannot rest or be happy until that person acknowledges his or her wrongdoing or seems to suffer for it. Unfortunately, we cannot change another person or make other people feel anything without their participation, so putting off our own happiness or well-being until the other becomes remorseful is a futile exercise.

We have to accept that it takes at least two people for a relationship to happen. If one of those chooses to opt out fully, then we have no choice but to continue our lives without that person. We are in charge of our own emotional ground, and the truth is that no one can make us feel anything without our acquiescence. The sooner we let go of the other person, the sooner we begin the road to recovery. This means letting go of thinking about the person all the time – perhaps limiting ourselves to talking about him or her for half an hour a day, and definitely not following the person on Facebook or other social media. Commit to putting your energy into yourself, surround yourself with people you like and gradually your sense of self and wholeness will return.

It is possible to love someone and let him or her go. If

you know that your relationship was good and could have been lifelong, but your partner opted out, you can continue to hold on to your truth while allowing your partner the right to leave. Do not feel you have to turn him or her into something bad to make sense of the separation, as this will destroy your faith in your judgement and perception. You have the right to have understanding from and conversations with your ex-partner until you feel you have all the truth about the situation – but then the letting go begins. Understand that you are fully in charge of what you feel, accept what is happening and engage with life as it presents itself today. This is the pathway to resilience.

Epilogue

How do we find enduring love?

Some of how we find enduring love remains a mystery, but we have learned a lot from both research and experience. Research clearly shows that the starting point has to be ourselves and developing characteristics that enhance our chances of finding and keeping enduring love. These characteristics include self-awareness, courage, decision-making and good judgement. Habit plays an important role, in the sense of both breaking old habits and creating new ones of honesty, risk-taking and resilience. An equation for romantic love is put forward as follows: kindness + loyalty + fairness + lust = romantic love. The four concepts making up romantic love in this equation are the everyday actions that keep love alive. It also has to be recognised that some sacrifice is involved in committing to a long-term relationship. Enduring love requires us to put the other person first and to give up our singledom for the relationship, while at all times not losing sight of our own needs and development.

Seeking a partner – either as a single person or as someone emerging from a separation – can be fraught with difficulties, and using online apps or websites seems to be the way forward in our modern world. Using the advice and experience of others is strongly recommended, but above all it is necessary not to give up too early, but to persevere and hone your skills in deciphering who might be a suitable partner. Attraction and confidence are closely linked, and once the date has been set up, the most important thing is to be yourself, express yourself honestly and not be afraid either to suggest another date or end the engagement; all these are actions that support self-regard. We often repeat mistakes from the past, and we can tackle these by being clear about the traits we are looking for in a partner and challenging ourselves to follow our aims and not our patterns. We need to be conscious and careful of what we practise, otherwise years can go by and somehow we still expect something other than what we are practising to happen.

The beginning of a relationship is the time to set in motion those traditions and traits that will support the relationship through its lifetime. Keeping an eye on insecurity, letting go of negative thoughts and committing at the right time and at the right pace are all important steps to take at this time. Being conscious of social groups and not isolating yourself as a couple is crucial, as many demands will be made on the relationship. Often, careers are expanding and there might be a demand for living in different countries or towns; this puts a strain on the burgeoning relationship. Friends can take some of the emotional pressure down a notch and give the relationship some breathing space.

Once a relationship is started, how couples fight seems to be the measure of whether they will stay together or separate, and it is worth noting that the 'Four Horsemen' – criticism, contempt, defensiveness and stonewalling – are all disastrous in arguments. However, if couples follow the rules in the exercise section 'How to argue better', they will be able to deal with any conflict in a constructive manner and move on, without permanently damaging the relationship – there is no doubt that if couples practise all the rules in the practical advice section, sainthood is on the way! Some reflection on the traits garnered from our families can also be very useful, as it can save repeated arguments and target the right thing in an altercation.

Intimacy and affection are the glue that keeps relationships on track. While opportunities for intimacy are outlined, the wisdom many people expressed, which is a useful general guideline for all couples, is to 'use it or lose it'. Eroticism is often the magic and mystery in a relationship, and giving time and energy to this can only be a good thing. We love spontaneity, but during the frantic years it is probably routine that keeps the intimacy engine running. No-sex relationships are common, but having the courage to talk and reflect on this is already a foray into intimacy. If sexual difficulties or divergent sexual desires are being encountered, then these need to be addressed not ignored. Likewise, if porn is an issue in your relationship, or you feel that it is a problem that is preventing you from forming long-term relationships – and there is in society as a whole a growing sense that porn can have a negative effect on both individuals and relationships – then this needs to be addressed. Discussion across the board is suggested, but again this will require courage and confidence – qualities on which we are already working.

It is important to realise that not all relationships will succeed or survive, and we need to avoid becoming stuck in a rut through fear or habit. Saucer-effect relationships – which might be described as the relationships of the 'I love you but I'm not in love with you' type of couple – are symptomatic of this. Such relationships are very difficult, in that they are not bad enough for the couple to separate but not good enough for them to commit fully, thus leaving everyone in limbo waiting for a crisis to instigate change. A seven-year review system is useful in this sort of situation, but the couple would need to agree to and understand this early in the relationship. Break-ups happen, and often these are not foreseen and can be devastating. They can leave both parties grief-stricken, and it can take a long time for people to re-emerge into the world of function and happiness.

One of the more common types of crisis that can cause a break-up is an affair. Affairs do not always signal the end of a relationship, but they always bring suffering and betrayal into the couple or family. When an affair happens, it is a good idea for the couple not to make life decisions immediately, but instead to wait until they understand all the information about the cause of the affair. This might take some time, as the hurt and defensiveness can be overwhelming. Getting outside help to have real discussions is probably a good idea, and – if a break-up is inevitable – mediation is a process whereby an agreeable outcome is possible.

Developing resilience – all the way from taking the risk of rejection when asking someone out through the tough times when the relationship is at risk – is a personal task. It takes resilience to stay in a relationship when things are not going well, to challenge both ourselves and our partner to be better people, and to take responsibility for our own selves. We often have the idea that it is our partner's job to make us happy, but really this is our own task. Knowing that we are responsible for our own feelings is key to having a good relationship; even if our partner does not appreciate this, the effect on us should be immediately enriching.

We have our whole lives to engage in relationships, to be curious, daring and adventurous. Rather than thinking we need to have everything sorted or 'fixed', we should take the attitude of seeing the relationship journey as an opportunity for further development and enhancement. In the many observations from participants about why their relationships have endured, the reasons include shared meaning, good arguments, commitment and laughing. It seems that the small moments and gestures have a very extensive effect, and turning towards your partner in these moments is relationship-enhancing. Remembering this could help develop and enhance your relationships too.

We will be able to recognise and even practise many – if not all – of the suggestions in this book on various occasions in our own lives. The challenge is to keep this knowledge as something practical and ongoing. It is a very powerful thing to know that you have the potential to do something even in the most difficult of situations or relationships. Having someone by our side, who bears witness to our lives and to whom we do the honour of being ourselves, is worth every inch of the journey. In the words of Elizabeth Gilbert, 'To be fully seen by somebody, then, and be loved anyhow – this is a human offering that can border on miraculous.'[1]

1   Gilbert, E., *Committed: A Sceptic Makes Peace with Marriage*, quoted in Gottman, J. M., *Principia Amoris: The New Science of Love* (Routledge, New York, 2015), p. 194.

Practical advice and exercises

#1 How to argue better

- Ground yourself: pause/breathe and remember your aim is to be heard and understood.

- Start with a question to lessen the aggression, for example: 'Are you up for a difficult discussion?'

- Own your feelings, for example: 'I'm feeling very strong about this issue and so I might come across as angry.'

- Remember the relationship, for example: 'I'm always going to have your back and this issue will not change that.'

- Humour: a light, optimistic approach will get you a long way towards being understood.

- Listen: if your partner feels understood, there is a far greater chance they will be interested in hearing your side of things.

#2 Self-awareness: knowing the state you are in and grounding yourself

- Find somewhere quiet and sit with your feet on the ground and your back straight.

- Close your eyes (or look at a single point on the floor).

- Feel your feet on the floor and the weight of your body as it sits.

- Be conscious of where your breathing is and gently pull it right down to the base of your spine.

- Continue to follow your breath.

- Give attention to taste and smell.

- Let your attention go to listening and go right out to the furthest sound.

- Do this for two minutes and you will be grounded in self-awareness.

- When you are grounded, your mind will be fully present and your body relaxed.

- Then ask yourself what is in front of you that needs attention.

#3 Overcoming fear

- Fear is mostly based on our idea of 'What might happen if …?' It creates tension and restricts our mental capacities of judgement and decision-making.

- Up to the point of fear we are in our comfort zones, and beyond that we are uncomfortable and anxious.

- Panic sets in if we are too far away from our comfort zones.

- Challenge fear by going to the edge of comfort every day.

- Speak or act in a way that creates some fear (but not too much), and then calm yourself down by breathing.

- For example, if you fear speaking publicly, try asking a question at a meeting or group.

- Do this every day and you will grow courage.

#4 Accessing intelligence

- Our intelligence is natural to us and the issue is in accessing it.

- Mostly it is blocked by fears, inner commentary, past experience or worry about the future.

- When we respond from these negative inner thoughts, we lose our capacity for good judgement, reason and creativity.

- We need to quieten the thoughts so that our natural capacity for intelligence can work.

- Quieten thoughts by being present, focus on the senses (sight, sound, touch, taste and smell) and take several breaths.

- If you are very agitated, do something physical before tackling the problem.

- Playing music, cooking or gardening, for example, will quieten your mind by focusing it in action, and then your intelligence will have more freedom to work.

#5 Developing confidence

- All children are born confident, assuming they are the centre of the universe.

- As we grow we get messages that challenge the idea that we are so wonderful.

- Gradually that confident core is covered by beliefs and ideas that we are not good enough, smart enough, beautiful enough or wealthy enough.

- We need to see these beliefs as blocks to our confidence and let them go.

- True confidence is to be happy being yourself, in your own skin, right now.

- It expresses itself in honesty and openness, and these are keys to confidence.

- For example, if you find you are feeling apprehensive and your body is tense, check what idea or notion is accompanying the tension, then let it go and engage with the situation. This will improve confidence.

#6 Decision-making

- When we make a decision that works, we follow it all the way.

- However, most of the time we try to implement something and fail.

- If possible, we should try to follow our decisions with body, mind and heart.

- If I say I will turn up at something, then my body should be there and my thinking should not try to get me out of it.

- For example, if I say yes to a birthday party, I turn up for it, even if another more exciting offer has come along.

- We often use fear to make decisions and while we need some fear (for example to drive under the speed limit), using only fear is not a good thing for us.

- Asking 'Is this good for me now?' is a good marker, as is 'Will more people benefit from this decision?'

- If we make good small decisions now, the future and the harder decisions will be easier to make.

#7 Attention

- The reason we find giving attention so difficult is distraction and our minds grabbing onto anything other than what we are doing.

- The key to attention is keeping focused on what is happening by using the senses.

- If you are on the phone, only listen to the voice and don't try to do other things.

- If you are on a computer, feel your fingers on the keyboard or eyes on the screen.

- If someone is in front of you, stop and listen.

- Very few of us can multitask well, and it costs us time and effort in the long run.

- Give those close to you the honour of your full attention for the few minutes it takes to figure out the state they are in.

#8 Gradual sensualisation exercises

- This exercise needs to be planned and deliberate, but be aware that this might make it awkward and will challenge the idea that sex or sensuality should always be spontaneous.

- Start with twenty-minute sessions twice a week with your partner.

- Begin with non-sexual sensual activities, for example, massage, sharing a bath with fragrant oils, etc.

- The exercises should be creative, fun and include all the senses. The idea is to retrain the body to be focused on the pleasure of the senses and to let go of the fear of failure, boredom, etc.

- Move to sexual sensual touching – no penetration.

- Focus on your senses, not on the result.

- If your mind starts to comment or worry – go back to your senses.

- Aim to be in the present, with no past/future/aim/expectation/fear/worry.

#9 Twenty-minute question-and-listening exercise

- Start with ten minutes where one part of the couple asks questions *only* – the other person answers fully. Over time move to twenty minutes per session.

- Decide how often – probably twice a week initially.

- Decide when and where this should happen.

- Take it in turns to be the questioner, possibly on different days.

- The outcome will be better if the topic is important to the person/relationship.

- Agree to honesty and no conversation or comments during this time.

- There is no need for resolution; it can be picked up again in the future.

#10 Sexual messages lifeline

- Represent on paper the 'messages' you have received (or things you have learned) to do with sex. These may be about information, sexual identity, sexual behaviour, responsibilities or expectations, among other things. The representation may be in words, pictures, diagrams or symbols.

- Messages may have been verbal or non-verbal (what is not said may be as important as what is said), and may have come from parents, siblings, peers, the media. They begin at birth and go on being received.

- Divide the 'messages' into three groups:

  1. those that no longer affect your life;
  2. those that are still significant and affect life negatively;
  3. those that are still significant and affect life positively.

- Share with your partner how your life is affected by these messages and what changes you would like to make.

Bibliography

Buchanan, D., *Meeting Your Match* (Carlton Books, London, 2015)

Butler, K., 'The Art & Science of Love', *Psychotherapy Networker*, Sept/Oct 2006, pp. 29–39

Chopra, D. (ed.), *The Love Poems of Rumi* (Harmony Books, New York, 1998)

'Claire: Divorce is about Growth and Change', in 'Divorced Ireland: The Readers Write', News Review, *The Irish Times*, 24 January 2015

De Botton, A., *How to Think More about Sex* (Pan Macmillan, London, 2012)

Doherty, K., 'Effects of Accessing Sexually Explicit Online Materials on Young Irish Males' Sexual Attitudes, Knowledge and Behaviours' (Masters in Psychological Science thesis University of Limerick, unpublished, 2013)

Finkel, E. J., Eastwick, P. W., Karney, B. R., Reis, H. T. and Sprecher, S., 'Dating in a Digital World', *Scientific American Mind*, Vol. 23, No. 4, Sept/Oct 2012, pp. 26–33

Gabb, J., Klett-Davies, M., Fink, J. and Thomae, M., 'Findings, Executive Summary', *Enduring Love? Couple Relationships in the 21st Century* (Open University Press, Milton Keynes, 2013)

Gaddam, S. and Ogas, O., *A Billion Wicked Thoughts: What the World's Largest Experiment Reveals about Human Desire* (Plume, New York, 2012)

Gaffney, M., 'Marriage Just Isn't What It Used to Be', *The Irish Times*, 28 March 2015

Gallacher, D. and Gallacher, J., 'Are Relationships Good for Your Health?', *Student British Medical Journal* (2011), http://student.bmj.com/student/view-article.html?id=sbmj.d404 (accessed 28 January 2014)

Goleman, D., *Emotional Intelligence* (Bantam Books, New York, 1995)

Gottman, J., *Principia Amoris: The New Science of Love* (Routledge, New York, 2015)

Gottman, J. and Schwartz Gottman, J., 'Lessons from the Love Lab: The Science of Couples Therapy', *Psychotherapy Networker*, Nov/Dec 2015, pp. 37–52

Gottman, J. and Silver, N., *The Seven Principles for Making Marriage Work* (Orion, London, 2007)

Henriques, S. M., *God Can Handle It ... Marriage* (Walnut Grove, Nashville, 2010)

Holmquist, K., 'Divorce, Irish Style', Weekend Review, *The Irish Times*, 17 January 2015

Holmquist, K., 'How to Find Love Online', *The Irish Times*, 10 February 2015

Holmquist, K., 'Let's Talk about Sex: The Full Survey Results', *The Irish Times*, 30 June 2015

Holmquist, K., 'When Porn Becomes a Problem', Weekend Review, *The Irish Times*, 8 August 2015

Maltz, W. and Maltz, L., *The Porn Trap* (HarperCollins, New York, 2010)

Marshall, A., *I Love You but I'm Not in Love with You: Seven Steps to Saving Your Relationship* (Bloomsbury, London, 2007)

Murphy, T., *The Challenge of Retirement* (Orpen Press, Dublin, 2014)

Natsal-3, 'The National Survey of Sexual Attitudes and Lifestyles, UK, 2010–2012', www.natsal.ac.uk

O'Morain, P., 'That's Men: "Revenge Porn" could be classified in law as a form of cyberbullying', Health Section, *The Irish Times*, 25 November 2014

O'Morain, P., 'That's Men: Relationships, like Artichokes, require Pause for Thought', Health Section, *The Irish Times*, 7 July 2015

Portner, M., 'The Orgasmic Mind', *Scientific American Mind*, Special Collection, 2009, pp. 27–31

Robbins, T., *Still Life with Woodpecker* (Bantam Books, New York, 1980)

Sales, N. J., 'Tinder is the Night', *Vanity Fair,* September 2015

Singh, R., 'Enduring Love? Couple Relationships in the 21st Century. Clinical Implications. Feedback', *Journal of the Family Therapy Association of Ireland,* Summer 2015, pp. 70–75

Sweeney, T., 'It's Complicated: The Truth about Women and Porn', *The Irish Times,* 20 January 2015

Tashiro, T., *The Science of Happily Ever After: What Really Matters in the Quest for Enduring Love* (Harlequin, Don Mills, 2014)

Zilbergeld, B., *The New Male Sexuality* (revised edition, Bantam Books, New York, 1999)

SUGGESTED FURTHER READING
Mindfulness

De Mello, A., *Awareness* (Image Publishing/Random House, London, 1990)

Gilbert, P., *The Compassionate Mind* (Constable, London, 2009)

Kabat-Zinn, J., *Full Catastrophe Living: Using the Wisdom of Your Body and Mind to Face Stress, Pain and Illness* (Piatkus, London, 1990)

Kabat-Zinn, J., *Wherever You Go, There You Are: Mindfulness Meditation in Everyday Life* (Piatkus, London, 1994)

Kabat-Zinn, J., *Coming to Our Senses: Healing Ourselves and the World through Mindfulness* (Piatkus, London, 2005)

Mace, C., *Mindfulness and Mental Health: Therapy, Theory and Science* (Routledge, New York, 2008)

Nhat Hanh, T., *Peace is Every Step: The Path of Mindfulness in Everyday Life* (Rider & Co., London 1995)

Tolle, E., *The Power of Now: A Guide to Spiritual Enlightenment* (Namaste Publishing, Vancouver, 1997)

Williams, M. and Penman, D., *Mindfulness: A Practical Guide to Finding Peace in a Frantic World* (Piatkus, London, 2011)

Sexuality

Berman, J. and Berman, L., *For Women Only: A Revolutionary Guide to Overcoming Sexual Dysfunction and Reclaiming Your Sex Life* (Henry Holt, New York, 2001)

Foley, S., Kope, S. A. and Sugrue, D. P., *Sex Matters for Women: A Complete Guide to Taking Care of Your Sexual Self* (Guilford Press, New York, 2002)

Friday, N., *My Secret Garden: Women's Sexual Fantasies* (Simon & Schuster, New York, 1973)

Friday, N., *Men in Love* (Arrow, London, 1980)

Kahr, B., *Sex and the Psyche* (Penguin, London, 2014)

Marshall, A. G., *How Can I Ever Trust You Again? Infidelity: From Discovery to Recovery in Seven Steps* (Bloomsbury, London, 2010)

Mental Health

Bates, T., *Depression: The Common Sense Approach* (Gill & Macmillan, Dublin, 1999)

Beattie, M., *Codependent No More* (Hazelden Publishing, Centre City 1986)

Burns, D. D., *The Feeling Good Handbook: Using the New Mood Therapy in Everyday Life* (William Morrow, New York, 1989)

Butler, G., *Overcoming Social Anxiety and Shyness – A Self-Help Guide using Cognitive Behavioural Techniques* (Robinson, London, 1999)

Gaffney, M., *Flourishing* (Penguin Ireland, Dublin, 2011)

Kennerley, H., *Overcoming Anxiety: A Self-Help Guide Using Cognitive Behavioural Techniques* (Robinson, London, 1997)

Levine, A. and Heller, R., *Attached* (Tarcher, New York, 2012)

Lindenfield, G., *Self Esteem Bible* (HarperCollins, London, 2014)

Ruiz, D. M., *The Four Agreements: A Practical Guide to Personal Wisdom* (Amber-Allen Publishing, San Rafael, 1997)

Seligman, M., *Learned Optimism: How to Change Your Mind and Your Life* (Vintage Books, New York, 2006)

Tubridy, Á., *When Panic Attacks* (Gill & Macmillan, Dublin, 2008)